PETER PAN

By JM Barrie

Devised by the Companies

OBERON BOOKS
LONDON ·

WWW.OBERONBOOKS.COM

J M Barrie, *Peter Pan*
and Great Ormond Street Hospital

'The moment you doubt whether you can fly,
you cease forever to be able to do it...'

JM Barrie, *Peter Pan in Kensington Gardens*

James Matthew Barrie's start in life was inauspicious. Born in Kirriemuir, Scotland in 1860, he was the ninth of ten children and the son of a weaver. He could have followed in the footsteps of his older siblings and pursued a teaching career but Barrie's faith, both in himself and in the alchemy of the imagination, took him further than even he dreamed. It is no accident that the notion of belief runs through *Peter Pan*, like a place name through a stick of rock: it is belief which enables the children to fly and belief that saves Tinker Bell's life. One of Peter's defining and most charming characteristics is that 'to him, make-believe and true were exactly the same thing'.

As a young child Barrie had good reason to dedicate himself to the transformative emotional power of make-believe. The death of his elder brother David, when Barrie was six, left an indelible mark on his family and his mother in particular, who had always favoured the elder boy. The young James Barrie desperately tried to fill the void, copying David's mannerisms and even dressing up as his brother in a tireless effort to lift his mother out of her depression. She found comfort in the invented tales with which Barrie entertained her, as well as in the notion that David would always be her little boy, never growing up and therefore never leaving her behind to enter adulthood.

In *Peter Pan* Barrie found a literary expression for these formative experiences exploring every child's natural compulsion towards independence, coupled with their innate suspicion of the grown up world and its responsibilities. Mothers, in this context, are at once lambasted and mythologized, providing succor and injury in almost equal measure. This isn't just the case for Peter and the other children – even Hook is afraid of the power of maternal love. When Captain Hook is confronted with the dangerous fact that one day the crocodile's clock will run down, and, later, with the idea that Peter is being protected by a mother's watchful eye, his response is identical: 'Ay, that is the fear that haunts me'.

At the same time as Barrie was growing up in Scotland, many miles away in London the Hospital for Sick Children, later to be known as Great Ormond Street Hospital, was also in its infancy. Dr Charles West, driven by the shockingly high level of infant mortality in the capital, founded the hospital starting with just ten beds in a townhouse. From its earliest years, founder Dr Charles West ran fundraising campaigns to keep developing and expanding this important resource. His endeavour depended on the support of luminaries including Queen Victoria and Charles Dickens and the cause quickly generated widespread interest as well as charitable donations from the public.

After graduating from Edinburgh University, Barrie moved to London and he married celebrated actress Mary Ansell, although they had no children and later divorced. He produced several novels, soon establishing himself as a successful author. In 1897, during a walk in Kensington Gardens, Barrie encountered Sylvia Llewelyn Davies and her sons with whom he developed an inspiring lifelong friendship. Barrie and the young Llewelyn Davies boys, especially George, Jack and Peter, created imaginary worlds together, often performing their invented tales for the rest of the family. After their father's untimely death Barrie provided the children with financial support and when Sylvia also passed away Barrie became a guardian to all five of the boys. The nature of loss is a constant theme in Barrie's work and in *Peter Pan*, through the lens of the children's adventures, we catch glimpses of the parlous adult world. We constantly feel the threat of tragedy lapping at the shores of the Neverland.

Although Peter Pan's story was rooted in Barrie's early life, his relationship with the Llewelyn Davies boys provided further inspiration and much of his impetus. He later referred to all five Llewelyn Davies boys in a dedication, saying he 'made Peter by rubbing the five of you violently together as savages with two sticks produce a flame. That is all Peter is – the spark I got from you.' The narrative as we know it today, emerged gradually over a number of years, and when Peter Pan first appeared on stage in 1904 he was instantly loved by adults, children and critics alike. The character Barrie introduced in his novel as a 'lovely boy, clad in skeleton leaves', cast his spell on audiences throughout the early twentieth century and his story became all the more poignant during the traumatic years of the First World War, in which George Llewelyn Davies was one of the many young men to lose their lives.

Barrie was not only a friend to the Llewelyn Davies children. He also believed in the importance of Dr West's work on behalf of the children of London, and was a supporter of Great Ormond Street Hospital for many years. Amongst other things, Barrie arranged for the cast of the West End production to perform for patients and staff at the hospital itself, and the tradition of cast visits endures to this day. But it was in 1929 that *Peter Pan*'s magic made an unprecedented leap from the realm of fiction into reality when Barrie generously gave his copyright to Great Ormond Street Hospital. From that moment on, all the proceeds from his most famous creation would benefit the Hospital and its patients. What Barrie could not have foreseen was just how enduring his gift would be and how many lives it would touch.

In recognition of J M Barrie's generosity and the exceptional work of the Hospital itself, the House of Lords in 1988 sprinkled more fairy dust over Great Ormond Street Hospital: they voted overwhelmingly for a special clause in the UK's Copyright Designs and Patents Act giving the Hospital the right to a royalty in perpetuity within the UK. Thus the story of Peter and Wendy's adventures in Neverland with Michael and John, Tinker Bell and the Lost Boys, the infamous Captain Hook and the ticking crocodile, not only continues to enchant children and adults alike – it also helps make Great Ormond Street Hospital the extraordinary place that it is today.

During the twentieth century Great Ormond Street Hospital has grown exponentially both in size and reach. It is now one of the world's leading children's hospitals and helps young people not just throughout the UK but worldwide, through treatments and the pioneering research which it undertakes, as well as by providing exceptional support to patients and their families.

Just as Barrie continued to tinker with Peter's story over several years, The Boy Who Would Not Grow Up has also inspired new artistic work across a variety of mediums. But the spirit of Peter Pan, and his belief in the extraordinary, does not just exist in our imaginations: it is embodied in the work that goes on every day at Great Ormond Street Hospital, it is drawn on by the children and families who have been touched by that work and it lives in the spirit of the hospital's supporters, past and present, all of whom share the belief that each contribution they make, no matter how large or small, can make a difference.

Sarah Wolf, *Peter Pan* Director, Great Ormond Street Hospital Children's Charity, 2016.

A version of this text first appeared in the programme for this production of *Peter Pan* at the National Theatre in London, November 2016

Peter Pan is a co-production between the National Theatre and Bristol Old Vic. It was first performed on 26 November 2012 at Bristol Old Vic; and a new production opened in the Olivier Theatre at the National on 2 December 2016.

Tinker Bell / Curly / Pirate **Saikat Ahamed**
Ensemble **Suzanne Ahmet**
John **Marc Antolin**
Musician **Benji Bower**
Musician **Will Bower**
Tiger Lily / Slightly / Pirate **Lois Chimimba**
Musician **Richie Crago**
Twin One / Pirate / Ensemble **Laura Cubitt**
Ensemble **Phoebe Fildes**
Hook / Mrs Darling **Anna Francolini**
Musician **Ruth Hammond**
Smee / Mr Darling / Twin Two / Ensemble **Felix Hayes**
Peter Pan **Paul Hilton**
Ensemble **John Leader**
Jane / Nibs / Pirate **Amaka Okafor**
Michael **John Pfumojena**
Nana / Tootles / Pirate **Ekow Quartey**
Ensemble **Jessica Temple**
Ensemble **Dan Wheeler**
Wendy **Madeleine Worrall**
Other parts played by members of the Company

With special thanks to **Sophie Thompson** *for creative input and for developing the roles of Hook and Mrs Darling*

Understudies
Suzanne Ahmet (Hook/Mrs Darling/Tiger Lily), **Phoebe Fildes** (Wendy/Jane), **John Leader** (Tinker Bell/Curly/Nana/Tootles), **Jessica Temple** (John/Michael/Twin One), **Dan Wheeler** (Peter Pan/Mr Darling/Smee/Twin Two)

Professional Counterweighters
Kieran Gonzalez, Maurycy Kowalski, Barnaby Wreyford

Director **Sally Cookson**
Dramaturg **Mike Akers**
Set Designer **Michael Vale**
Costume Designer **Katie Sykes**
Lighting Designer **Aideen Malone**
Music/Music Director **Benji Bower**
Sound Designer **Dominic Bilkey**
Movement Director **Dan Canham**
Aerial Director **Gwen Hales**
Puppetry Designer and Director **Toby Olié**
Fight Directors **Rachel Bown-Williams**
and **Ruth Cooper-Brown** of Rc-Annie Ltd
Associate Director **Ellen Havard**
Assistant Aerial Director **Tom Ratcliffe**
Company Voice Work **Jeannette Nelson**
and **Charmian Hoare**

Production Manager **David Stothard**
Casting **Juliet Horsley**
Stage Manager **Shane Thom**
Deputy Stage Manager **Nik Haffenden**
Assistant Stage Managers **Ian Connop** and **Jo Phipps**
Deputy Production Manager **Richard Eustace**
Puppetry Captain **Laura Cubitt**
Project Draughting **Oliver Cooper**
Digital Art **Daniel Radley-Bennett**
Costume Supervisor **Ashley Holtom**
Costume Buyer **Holly Henshaw**
Wigs, Hair & Make-up Supervisor **Renata Hill**
Prop Supervisor **Rebecca Johnston**
Prop Buyer **Kemey Lafond**
Puppet Supervisor **Daisy Beattie**
Lighting Supervisor **Breandan Ansdell**
Lighting Programmer **Henri Charlton**
Production Sound Engineer **Alex Caplen**
Sound Operator **Joel Price**
Rigging Supervisor **Matt Wheeler**
Automation **Jo Colley**
Construction Supervisor **Paul Sheppard**
Scenic Art Supervisor **Daina Ennis**
Assistant to the Designer **Sarah June-Mills**
Production Photographer **Steve Tanner**

Prologue

WENDY in the present, an adult with a daughter, JANE. She enters JANE's bedroom, tidying, picking up toys. She picks up a teddy and sits on the bed. It sparks a memory.

WENDY: All children grow up. They soon know they will grow up, and the way that I knew was this. One day when I was two years old I was playing in the garden. I plucked a flower and ran with it to my mother. I suppose I must have looked rather delightful, for she put her hand to her heart and cried 'Oh why can't you remain like this forever?' That was all that passed between us on the subject. But after that I knew that I must grow up. You always know after you're two. Two is the beginning of the end.

As WENDY recalls each character, they come into the space, they are all their past selves, on the night PETER PAN first arrives in the nursery.

WENDY: In this house, at number fourteen, there used to live…my mother.

MRS DARLING enters looking for her earring.

MRS DARLING: George? I can't find my earrings. The pink ones. Shape of a star.

WENDY: My father.

MR DARLING enters in a panic.

MR DARLING: Mary, it's twenty to seven. I don't mean to rush you. I'm just telling you the time.

WENDY: My brother John.

JOHN enters, crowing.

JOHN: I just got a shilling for eating all my dinner!

WENDY: And my youngest brother Michael.

MICHAEL enters, crawling in like a commando.

MICHAEL: I just can't go on without the bravest teddy…Ah! *(He sees the teddy on the bed and grabs it.)* There he is!

WENDY: And reigning above us all was…

Act One

SCENE ONE: THE DARLING NURSERY

WENDY is now also back in time on the night when PETER PAN first arrives. She calls to NANA, the nurse. She is a Newfoundland dog.

WENDY: …Nana!

NANA barks from off stage. WENDY and the children pat their knees trying to get her to come in.

WENDY: Nana! Come on girl! Come on!

NANA continues barking for a while before entering. She is able to speak but the other characters don't understand her.

NANA: What? What do you want? Look at the state of this room! This was tidy half an hour ago! Right it's bed time. Come on. Bed!

WENDY: Nana! Sit!

NANA: I don't have time for this I…

WENDY: Nana! Sit!

NANA: Alright alright alright I'll do it, but then it's bed time okay?

(NANA sits, resignedly.) Look I sat, aren't I a good girl? Come on, bed, bed, bed, bed, bed.

NANA tries to chivvy the children into bed.

WENDY: Good girl Nana. Now beg.

NANA: Beg?

WENDY: Beg Nana.

NANA: Beg? Beg? You want me to beg? Are you serious? I do not beg for anyone.

WENDY calls to JOHN on the bed.

WENDY: John, give me the biscuit.

JOHN hands WENDY a biscuit from his pyjama pocket.

WENDY: Do you want a little biscuit?

NANA is powerless to resist. She goes to WENDY and kneels down, panting and holding up her front paws.

NANA: I'll do anything for a biscuit.

WENDY: Good girl Nana!

JOHN throws a pillow from the bed on to the floor.

JOHN: Nana. Fetch!

NANA: Oh for crying out loud.

MICHAEL: Nana. Fetch!

NANA: Pillows do not live on the floor John.

WENDY: Come on Nana, fetch!

NANA: Fine. I'll fetch it.

NANA picks up the pillow and holds it up to show she has done the fetch command.

NANA: *(Underwhelmed.)* Oh look I picked up a pillow. Yay for me!

JOHN, MICHAEL and WENDY rush across to praise her.

CHILDREN: Good girl Nana, who's a good doggy?

They tickle Nana.

NANA: Oh, I like it, I like it, I like it, I like it, I like it. I don't like it! Bed time!

The CHILDREN back to the bed pillow fighting. MRS DARLING enters, dressed for her night out.

MRS DARLING: Nana, you are wonderful. What would we do without you? You look exhausted.

NANA: Exhausted doesn't even come close.

MRS DARLING crosses to the bed.

MRS DARLING: Come on now it's time to go to sleep, daddy and I have to go to this silly, silly party.

The CHILDREN look disappointed. They don't want her to go.

MRS DARLING: But…I suppose there might just be time for a little more of the story.

The CHILDREN are delighted and they all sit up in the bed. MRS DARLING calls NANA to join them by the bed.

MRS DARLING: Now, where did we get to?

WENDY: Cinderella was at the ball.

MICHAEL: She was dancing with the prince.

JOHN: No, no, no, no, she was leaving the ball.

MRS DARLING: Ah, that's right.

MR DARLING is up his ladder becoming increasingly frustrated with his tie.

MRS DARLING: The chimes of midnight had struck and Cinderella's glass slipper fell off as she hurtled down the steps of the palace.

She is interrupted by MR DARLING. He storms down the ladder having finally lost patience with his tie. He flounces across the stage muttering angrily. He throws the tie on the floor. He is only wearing one shoe.

MR DARLING: Arghhh! Stupid tie!

MRS DARLING: Is something the matter dear?

MR DARLING: Matter? This tie will not tie. Not round my neck. Round the bedpost, oh yes. Twenty times I have made it up round the bedpost, but round my neck, oh dear no, begs to be excused. I warn you Mary, that unless this tie is round my neck we don't go out to the party tonight, and if we don't go to the party tonight, I never go to the office again and if I don't go to the office again we will starve and our children will be thrown on to the streets.

He bursts into tears. The children look on anxiously.

MRS DARLING: Let me try dear.

She stands in front of him and starts tying the tie.

MRS DARLING: It's very simple. Over and under, round and through. There. It's all done.

The tie is on. MR DARLING is speechless with joy. He runs across to the children on the bed showing them the tie.

MR DARLING: She's done it! Hoopla!

ALL: Hoopla!

They all start bouncing in celebration. NANA tries to get MR DARLING off the bed and in doing so covers him in dog hair. Affronted, he tries to get NANA to sit.

MR DARLING: Nana! Nana! Sit Nana! Sit Nana! Sit! Sit! Sit!

NANA doesn't sit, she steps away from the bed and eyeballs him, growling. MR DARLING breaks first and moves away in a huff, brushing himself off as he goes.

MR DARLING: I do not like the noise that dog is making. Look she's covered me in hairs.

MRS DARLING: Let me brush you dear.

MR DARLING: I sometimes think Mary that it was a mistake having a dog for a nurse. Where is my shoe?

MR DARLING begins looking for the shoe. NANA begins settling the children into bed.

MRS DARLING: Nana is a treasure, we must keep her and I will tell you why.

MR DARLING looks for his shoe, crossing over the bed as he does so. MRS DARLING follows him, trying to get his attention but he remains preoccupied with the shoe.

My dear, when I came into this room tonight… *(To the children briefly as she crosses the bed.)* alright children

I'll be with you in a moment…*(Back to following MR DARLING.)* I saw a face at the window.

MR DARLING finds his shoe and puts it on.

MR DARLING: Aha!

MRS DARLING: It was the face of a little boy. He was trying to get in. This is not the first time I have seen him.

MR DARLING: Three floors up? Of course you did dear. Would you mind?

MR DARLING offers out his arms for her to put his cufflinks on.

MRS DARLING: Of course dear. The first time was a week ago. It was Nana's night out and I was drowsing by the fire when suddenly I felt a draught, as if the window were open. I looked round and I saw that boy – in the room.

MR DARLING: In the room?

MRS DARLING: I screamed, Nana rushed back and sprang at him. The boy leapt for the window. She pulled down the sash quickly but she was too late to catch him. The boy escaped but his shadow had not time to get out; down came the window and cut it clean off.

MR DARLING: Cut it clean off? Mary, why on Earth didn't you keep it?

MRS DARLING: I did. I rolled it up and put it in a drawer.

She fetches it from behind a ladder.

MRS DARLING: And here it is.

They unravel it and stretch it out. MR DARLING examines the shadow, finally interested.

MR DARLING: It is nobody I know, but he does look a scoundrel.

MRS DARLING: I think he comes back to get his shadow George.

MR DARLING takes the shadow, folds it up and puts it back where it came from, closing down the discussion. He is supremely aware of the time.

MRS DARLING: I dare say he does. I shall take this chap up to the British Museum on Monday and have him valued.

NANA rings a bell from the other ladder.

MR DARLING: Seven o'clock? We must be going!

MRS DARLING: Silly me. I forgot Michael's medicine time.

MICHAEL: No I won't take it.

MICHAEL is horrified. He crawls under the bed.

MR DARLING: Be a man Michael.

MRS DARLING: You can have a nice chocolate afterwards.

MICHAEL comes out, tempted by the offer.

MR DARLING: Stop pampering him, Mother. I take my medicine without a murmur.

MRS DARLING: Well then take a spoonful now as an example to Michael.

WENDY: I'll fetch it for you Father.

MR DARLING: Uh, no wait Wendy. There really is no need…

WENDY goes up one ladder to fetch the medicine. MRS DARLING fetches the chocolate from the other ladder.

MR DARLING: John it really is nasty stuff. That horrible, sticky, sweet kind.

JOHN: Be a man Father, it will soon be over.

WENDY returns with the medicine.

WENDY: I've been as quick as I could.

WENDY holds the medicine up to him.

MR DARLING: Michael first.

MICHAEL: Father's a cowardy custard.

MR DARLING: If you're so brave then you take it.

MICHAEL: No you take it.

MR DARLING: No you take it.

This stand-off builds until interrupted by WENDY.

WENDY: Why don't you both take it at the same time?

MRS DARLING: What a good idea.

MRS DARLING pours a spoonful of medicine and offers it to MR DARLING. NANA is poised in front of MICHAEL with his medicine.

MRS DARLING: Now sit down. Ready?

A look between MICHAEL and MR DARLING. They are both ready.

WENDY: One…two…three!

MICHAEL swallows his revolting medicine down, MR DARLING pretends to, but has really thrown it behind his back. JOHN spots what has happened and jumps up holding the offending spoon.

JOHN: Father hasn't taken his!

MRS DARLING: Oh George!

MICHAEL bursts into tears. Everyone gathers round him and cuddles him.

MRS DARLING: Have a chocolate.

MICHAEL is soothed a little by the chocolate.

MR DARLING: Oh that's right, coddle him! Nobody ever coddles me! Why would they, I am only the breadwinner, why should I be coddled? Why? Why? Why?

MRS DARLING: George! Apologise to Michael.

MR DARLING: I don't see why I should…

MRS DARLING: Will you do as you're told, George? Please?

He apologises sulkily.

MR DARLING: I'm sorry Michael.

MRS DARLING: Now take your medicine.

MR DARLING: Mary, is that really necessary?

NANA pours him a spoonful of medicine.

ALL: One…two…three.

She holds his nose to make him open his mouth. he swallows the medicine. he reacts violently, staggering across the stage, revolted by the taste.

MR DARLING: I need a Chocky! It's disgusting.

MR DARLING goes to get the chocolate but they are all gone. The children cheer.

ALL: Hoopla!

They romp again. MR DARLING breaks the mood.

MR DARLING: We are going to be late! Will you all please get into bed?

MR DARLING is almost breaking down again.

NANA: Bed time.

The children lie down.

MR DARLING: Oh you listen to her, do you? Am I the master in this house or is she? We're late for the party, I'm covered in dog hair, I've got a horrible taste in my mouth and it is all that canine's fault! The proper place for you is out in the yard.

MR DARLING drags NANA away and exits to chain her in the yard. The children are horrified and gather behind MRS DARLING, protesting.

MRS DARLING: *(To herself.)* George, remember what I said… about the boy.

The children continue complaining. MRS DARLING calms things down.

MRS DARLING: Now listen, Nana's going to be quite alright, a bit of fresh air will do her the world of good and when daddy and I get home I'll bring her in again, you don't have to worry. Be brave darlings.

MRS DARLING gets the children back to bed. NANA howls from the yard.

MICHAEL: Nana!?

JOHN: She sounds really unhappy.

WENDY: That is not her unhappy bark. That's her bark when she smells danger.

MRS DARLING: Danger! Are you sure, Wendy?

WENDY: Oh yes.

JOHN: Is anything there?

MRS DARLING looks out. A sound effect hints that there is something outside. MRS DARLING shuts down the anxiety.

MRS DARLING: Nothing at all. Only the moon and the stars. *(To herself.)* I wish I weren't going out tonight. *(To them.)* I'll light the nightlights. That's what I'll do.

She lights the nightlights with a match, one by one.

MICHAEL: Mother? Can anything harm us, after the nightlight is lit?

MRS DARLING: Nothing, precious. It is the watchful eye a mother leaves behind to guard her children.

MICHAEL: Mother, I'm glad of you.

MRS DARLING kisses MICHAEL on the cheek.

JOHN: Mother what about the story?

MRS DARLING: We will finish it tomorrow night.

She sings.

> *Go to sleep now,*
> *Close your eyes and dream,*
> *Safe in your home,*
> *I will be always here for you.*

Goodnight my darlings.

She exits. The children fall fast asleep in the bed.

The nightlights go out one by one.

SCENE TWO: PETER BREAKS THROUGH

A light appears on the screen behind the bed, moving across first to stage left; then back over to stage right. TINKER BELL enters from stage right and goes up the ladder.

She catches the light and it becomes a light orb in her hand.

She journeys this over to the bed, climbing up the back of it, examining first JOHN, then MICHAEL and WENDY. TINKER BELL speaks the fairy language. Only PETER can understand her. The English translations are in brackets.

TINKER BELL: Chad-O? Chaaad-O? *(Shadow? Shadow?)*

TINKER BELL spots something in the floor and climbs down into the trap.

Above the bed, PETER carefully cuts a slit in the screen. He puts his head through the hole looking for TINKER BELL.

PETER: Tinker Bell? Have you found it yet? Tinker Bell? Have you found my shadow?

He steps through into the nursery at the top of a ladder, looking around for TINKER BELL. He jumps down on to the head of the bed. He sees the shadow.

PETER: There you are. I've been looking for you.

The shadow comes to life on the bed. It jumps from the bed to the ladder as PETER comes down after it.

PETER: This is no time for silly games. Come here.

The shadow faces PETER. They play a mirroring game before PETER leaps at it and manages to grab it. There is a tug of war with the shadow trying to escape PETER's grasp. Eventually the shadow is subdued and PETER tries to stick back on to his foot.

PETER: Don't you ever do that again. Stick…stick…stick!

He gives up and begins to cry. WENDY is woken by the sound of his tears.

WENDY: Boy, why are you crying?

PETER: I wasn't crying.

WENDY: It looked like you were crying.

PETER makes an elaborate formal bow to WENDY. WENDY reciprocates.

PETER: What's your name?

WENDY: Wendy Moira Angela Darling. What's yours?

PETER: Peter Pan.

WENDY: Is that all?

PETER: It's enough.

WENDY: Didn't your mother give you any middle names?

PETER: I don't have a mother.

WENDY: Is that you why were crying?

PETER's focus returns to his lifeless shadow.

PETER: I wasn't crying. I was trying to just…

He goes back to the shadow, frustrated with it.

WENDY: You seem to have a problem with your shadow?

PETER: Yes.

WENDY: You have tried sewing?

PETER: What's sewing?

WENDY: Don't you know what sewing is?

PETER: Yes. Of course I do.

WENDY fetches her sewing box from under the bed.

WENDY: I was given this last Christmas. I opened it once, but only so they'd think I like it. I don't. I hate sewing. What colour thread would you like?

PETER: Green.

WENDY hands PETER a needle.

WENDY: There you are.

PETER takes the needle. Explores it.

PETER: That is very sharp. It's a fairy sword. En garde. Ch…
ch..ch…kwuh.

*He uses it to have a pretend swordfight, making the sounds
as he does so.*

WENDY: Are you trying to be funny?

PETER: No.

He goes across and starts sword fighting with the shadow.

WENDY: You don't know how to sew at all, do you?

PETER: Yes. Watch me sew. Ch…ch…ch, kwuh, kwuh.

WENDY: Oh I can see I'll have to do it. Give it here.

PETER hands over the needle.

WENDY: Sit.

PETER goes to sit on the floor.

WENDY: On the bed.

*PETER sits on the bed, WENDY kneels at his feet getting ready
to sew the shadow on.*

WENDY: With your shadow.

PETER gets the shadow and sits on the bed.

WENDY: Have you ever had something surgically re-attached?

PETER: No.

WENDY: Foot.

PETER gives her his foot.

WENDY: I dare say this will hurt a little.

PETER: I'm not frightened.

WENDY sews on the shadow. PETER is in agonising pain but trying hard not to show it.

WENDY: Other foot.

She sews the shadow on to the other foot with the same result. When she has finished, PETER is delighted and is totally focused on the shadow. One of the ensemble moves a spotlight into position for him.

PETER: Cock a doodle doo! Oh the cleverness of me! Oh Peter Pan! I am such a cocky lad!

He clicks his fingers and his shadow appears on the Kabuki curtain. PETER plays in the light making different shapes and crowing about his success.

A second light joins.

He makes bird shadows with his fingers.

PETER: Cock a doodle doo! Cock a doodle doo!

PETER clicks again and the lights disappear.

PETER: Did you see that?

WENDY retreats under the bedclothes, annoyed that he is taking all the credit.

PETER: Wendy? Moira? Angela? Darling?

WENDY springs out from under the covers.

WENDY: Cock a doodle doo, cock a doodle wotsit. You're so full of yourself. You're exactly like John when he manages to squeeze another shilling out of Mother and Father by pretending to be nice and you ask him what he's going to spend it on and he says 'only stupid people spend their money all at once. Sensible people set it aside in a savings account.' And Father says that's exactly what the government would say. And then I just want to hit John and then I'm the one who gets into trouble, which is so unfair because it was all John's fault in the first place and now you're behaving exactly like him, which is such a shame because in my dreams you were always so much fun. You've spoilt it now. You're a real disappointment.

She goes back under the covers.

PETER: Wow. Wow. Wendy. I can't help cock a doodle dooing when I'm pleased with myself. That's what I do. I'm Peter Pan. Wendy, I think that one girl is worth more than twenty boys.

WENDY comes back out from under the covers.

WENDY: Do you really mean that?

PETER: Yes I do.

WENDY: That's very nice of you to say. If you like I'll give you a kiss.

PETER: Yes please!

PETER holds out his hand for the kiss.

WENDY: Surely you know what a kiss is?

PETER: I will when you give it to me.

She goes back to the sewing box and gets a thimble, which she gives to him. He is impressed.

PETER: Shall I give you a kiss?

WENDY: Yes please.

PETER: Close your eyes. Close your eyes really tight.

WENDY does so. She is expecting a real kiss. Instead PETER holds a Neverland acorn up in front of her.

PETER: Now you can open them.

WENDY does so.

WENDY: Thank you. I'll put it in my chest pocket.

PETER: I'll put mine in my chest pocket.

From underneath the stage TINKER BELL is heard.

TINKER BELL: Peta, weer arr ooo? Peta? (*Peter? Where are you Peter?*)

PETER: Tink? Tink? Have you seen her? She's really tiny. She's my fairy.

WENDY: Fairy? Don't be so ridiculous. Nobody believes in fair…

PETER cuts her off before she can finish.

PETER: Shh…don't say that. Don't ever ever say that. Every time a child says I don't believe in … *(He can't say the word.)* somewhere in the world a *(He can't say the word.)* drops down dead.

TINKER BELL knocks from under the stage

TINKER BELL: Peta! Peta! Erre arr ooo Peta? Erre arr ooo? *(Peter! Peter! Where are you? Where are you?)*

TINKER BELL knocks again.

PETER: If you want to see a real fairy in action. Clap your hands. Clap your hands. Louder.

WENDY starts clapping, not feeling very sure why she is doing so.

WENDY: Peter, you're not trying to tell me there is a fairy in this room?

PETER opens the trap ready to get TINKER BELL out.

PETER: Three, two, one, out!

TINKER BELL bursts into the space with a tirade of abuse in the fairy language. PETER is able to translate.

TINKER BELL: Bride O la. Bride O la. off skuff ekas Peta! Bzzzzz, ewear eroo? fzzzz. Ma reanly dee id. Ma reanly dee id. *(Free at last. Free at last. What the hell, Peter! Where were you? I nearly died. I nearly died.)*

WENDY: Peter, what is the matter with her?

TINKER BELL: Me sufi arbora plonka, Peta. *(I've been stuck under the floorboards, Peter.)*

25

PETER: She's really upset, she's been trapped in the floorboards.

WENDY is overwhelmed with excitement.

WENDY: Peter, I want her!

TINKER BELL reacts with fierce contempt.

TINKER BELL: Oo geeb, fleecy, pusty, she bore. *(You big, hairy, ugly, cow.)*

PETER: Tinker Bell that is rude.

WENDY: What did she say?

PETER: Are you sure you want to know?

WENDY: Yes.

TINKER BELL encourages PETER to translate.

PETER: She…thinks…that you…are a …

TINKER BELL: Geeb.

PETER: …big

TINKER BELL: Fleecy.

PETER: …hairy

TINKER BELL: Pusty.

PETER: …ugly

TINKER BELL: She bore! She bore!

PETER: Girl.

WENDY: Well I rather expected she would be more polite.

More fairy abuse. TINKER BELL is really aggressive.

TINKER BELL: Paleet? Paleet? Harky meem glir bud. Tinker Bell, Zzzzb, minkin oo mizzy mizzy manky. Chunka she bore. Chunka she bore! *(Polite? Polite? Listen to me girlfriend, Tinker Bell is going to make your life a misery. Big cow. Big cow!)*

PETER: Tinker Bell I've warned you about that language. Right. We're leaving.

WENDY: Where are you going?

PETER: Back to the Lost Boys.

WENDY: Who are they?

PETER: They are the boys who fell out of their prams when their mothers weren't looking. I'm Captain.

WENDY: Aren't there any girls?

PETER: Of course not. Girls are much too clever to fall out of their prams.

WENDY: I think it's lovely the way you talk about girls. If you like you may give me a kiss.

PETER: I knew you'd want it back.

WENDY: No. I don't mean a kiss, I mean a thimble.

PETER: What's a thimble?

WENDY: I'll show you.

She kisses him.

PETER: Funny. Now shall I give you a thimble?

WENDY: Yes.

As PETER is about to 'thimble' her, WENDY lets out a scream, her hair has been pulled.

TINKER BELL: Zheee!! Pusty moom zzzzzz morta! Weed yank, weed yank, thimble thimble weed yank. *(What!!! That ugly bimbo is soooo dead. I'll rip your hair out, rip your hair out, thimble and I'll rip your hair out.)*

PETER: Tinker Bell says she's going to do that to you every time you give me a thimble.

WENDY: What have I ever done to you?

TINKER BELL: Eva done a u? Lok dee clow, glir bud. Peta, Peta, a vouchcous Neverland Peta! Folly chunka bore a BONG BONG BONG! *(Ever done to you? Talk to the hand girlfriend. Peter, Peter, let's go! Neverland Peter. Get the story first!)*

PETER: Alright Tink, yes. We just need to know the end of the story. Your mother was telling you a story, about a lady who turns into a pumpkin.

WENDY: You mean Cinderella.

PETER: Yes.

WENDY: She marries the prince and lives happily ever after.

PETER: I must get back and tell the boys before I forget.

PETER heads for the window.

WENDY: Don't you know that story?

PETER: I don't know any stories. None of us do. That's why I've been coming here. When the window is open I sit outside and listen, then I take the stories back for the boys. Except last time your mother shut the window halfway through and… I only came back to get my shadow.

PETER is leaving.

WENDY: Don't go Peter. I know such lots of stories.

PETER: You know stories. You know stories. You know stories.

He grabs her hand and draws her towards the window.

WENDY: Let me go.

PETER: Do you want to stay in your silly bed when you can be out flying with me?

WENDY: Fly? You can fly?

PETER: Yes. Fly away with me.

WENDY: I can't fly.

PETER: I'll teach you.

WENDY: Would you teach John and Michael too?

PETER: Yes. Of course.

WENDY wakes up JOHN and MICHAEL.

WENDY: John! Michael! Wake up. This is Peter Pan. He has come to teach us how to fly.

JOHN: Can you really fly?

PETER: Oh yes.

JOHN: Go on then.

> *PETER closes his eyes and lifts off. He jumps over the bed.*
> *MICHAEL and JOHN are amazed.*

MICHAEL: How did you do that?

PETER: Well it's simple. All you do is think of a wonderful
thought in your head and you will need...fairy string.

MICHAEL: I want a go.

PETER: Think of a wonderful thought!

MICHAEL: Mother's ginger biscuits.

> *Nothing happens.*

PETER: Think of a wonderful thought in your head and it will
help to lift you off the ground.

MICHAEL: Flying my kite on a windy day at the park.

> *MICHAEL lifts off the bed.*

MICHAEL: Woh!!! Woh!!! Look at me! I'm flying!!

> *He laughs delightedly.*

JOHN: My turn!

PETER: Think of a wonderful thought in your head!

JOHN: A wonderful thought? Playing football till tea time...

PETER: You need fairy string. Give me your hand. Wonderful
thoughts.

JOHN: Wonderful thoughts...catching fireflies in jam jars

> *JOHN is able to do a small jump.*

JOHN: ... Beating Father at chess

> *JOHN is able to do a bigger jump.*

JOHN: ...Beating Wendy at chess!

JOHN takes a few steps back and is able to do a big running jump.

WENDY: I think I'd like a go now, please.

PETER: Think wonderful thoughts and you will need fairy string.

WENDY: Yes, yes, I know, I need to use the fairy string.

WENDY: Sitting on John's head in the garage until he passed out… When Mother spent two months sewing me a dress and everyone said it was the prettiest…

WENDY lifts off a tiny bit.

WENDY: …The time when slugs came over the garden wall and ate all of Father's prize cucumbers.

WENDY goes further up in the air.

WENDY: … When my pet wolf walked out of the forest and asked if it could sleep at the end of my bed.

WENDY lifts high off the ground. They all lift off and fly simultaneously, playing in the air, doing turns and somersaults. PETER is on the bed watching them with delight.

MICHAEL: Peter how far can you fly?

PETER: Further than you can imagine.

JOHN: Let's fly out of the window!

MICHAEL: Yes, let's fly out of the window!

PETER: Let's fly out of the window!

WENDY comes back down.

WENDY: We are not flying out of the window.

PETER: Wendy, Wendy, you don't want to ride on the wind's back?

WENDY: I couldn't. Think of Mother.

PETER: You don't want to see pirates? You don't want to see mermaids swimming in the shallows?

WENDY: Mermaids? With tails?

PETER: Such long tails.

WENDY: I would love to see a mermaid.

PETER: Wendy out the window. Wendy out the window.

The boys join in chanting for WENDY.

WENDY: Alright! Let's fly out the window!

The ensemble enter with giant pieces of card. The children climb onto the bed.

PETER: First things first. Open the window.

They mime opening the sash window. The ensemble mirror this with their pieces of card. When the window opens they waft the cardboard as if it is getting windy.

PETER: Make your way to the ledge.

They step out on to the ledge.

PETER: Do not look down.

They immediately look down and jump with fright.

PETER: Ready? Second to the right and straight on till morning!

They all fly out of the window.

SCENE THREE: FLIGHT TO NEVERLAND

The Darling children are flying on the bed, suspended on their wires and leaning out over the edge. PETER and TINKER BELL alongside them on ladders.

The ensemble fold their giant pieces of card in half so they become the rooftops of houses. Two of the pieces of card make a window beneath the rooftops and there is a moment where we see MR and MRS DARLING framed by the window looking up and seeing the children fly away.

The ensemble change the rooftop cards for planets on long sticks. They move around the children revolving the planets. Comets fly past.

The planets disappear and the ensemble bring out clouds, which cluster around PETER and TINKER BELL. They lie down on them as if sitting on a sofa. They blow the clouds in front of the children. The children struggle to see past them and then blow them forwards.

The clouds turn dark, and it starts raining. PETER and TINKER BELL bring out watering cans and mime raining on the children.

Half of the ensemble pull out ribbons from under the bed and stretch them forward as if they are flying over the sea. Other members of the ensemble puppeteer sea birds, flitting above the waves.

PETER and TINKER BELL climb down their ladders a little way as if they have disappeared.

MICHAEL: Are we lost?

WENDY: Peter will know the way.

MICHAEL: Where is he?

JOHN: He's probably gone somewhere to show off.

WENDY: At least he's got something to show off about John. You couldn't fly until…

JOHN: How long have we been flying?

MICHAEL: Can we go back?

WENDY: How could we ever find our way back without him?

MICHAEL: I want Nana.

PETER and TINKER BELL return.

WENDY: Oh Peter! I knew you'd come back.

PETER: I'm sure I know you from somewhere…

WENDY: I'm Wendy.

PETER: Wendy! If you ever see me forgetting again then keep on saying to me 'I am Wendy' and then I'll remember.

A golden light floods the stage.

PETER: There it is!

WENDY: It's just as I imagined. John there's your lagoon.

JOHN: Look Michael, there's your cave!

MICHAEL: Wendy there's your wolf.

WENDY: Where?

JOHN: Just across the mysterious river.

PETER: That's Tiger Lily.

WENDY: Is she your friend?

PETER: She lives with the wolves. Do you want to go down and have an adventure now or would you like to have your tea first?

WENDY: Tea first.

JOHN: What kind of adventure?

PETER: Pirates! Shall we go down and kill one.

JOHN: Have you killed many?

PETER: Tons!

MICHAEL: Are there lots of them?

PETER: Hundreds! And their Captain is Hook.

WENDY: The deadliest pirate of them all.

PETER: She is the only pirate Blackbeard was afraid of.

MICHAEL: Is she big?

PETER: She is not as big as she was.

MICHAEL: How do you mean?

PETER: I cut her right hand off. Now she has an iron hook instead of a hand and she *claws* with it.

MICHAEL: You're very brave Peter.

PETER: That's why I am Captain. There's one thing that everyone who serves under me must promise. If ever we meet the pirates in open conflict, you leave Hook to me.

JOHN & MICHAEL: We promise.

PETER: That means you too Wendy.

WENDY: Alright.

JOHN: Look. The pirates are loading their cannon.

PETER: They've spotted us; We'll have to split up. We'll meet back down on the island. Hurry!

The air is suddenly rent by a huge explosion as the PIRATES fire their cannon. A lighting change puts them into silhouette and they all fall down screaming.

Act Two: The Neverland

There is a voiceover telling us that we have arrived in the Neverland.

V/O: Ladies and gentlemen, welcome to Neverland.

The Kabuki curtain across the stage falls and reveals the world inhabited by the Lost Boys.

They are bouncing around in the space on bungees, swings, bikes and prams, singing the LOST BOYS song:

> *Oober furry what's it,*
> *Doodle flanger whizzy werry woo,*
> *Giant butterflies and crocodiles,*
> *Oochi coochi woo woo,*
> *Oogie googie smelly botty bum.*

> *We are the Lost Boys we live in Neverland,*
> *We got here some time ago, we fell out of our prams,*
> *We are the Lost Boys, brave soldiers all,*
> *Ready to do battle when we hear our Captain call,*
> *We are the Lost Boys, best of friends to some,*
> *We're as tough as leather but we really miss our mums.*
> > *Really miss our mums…*
> > *Really miss our mums…*
> > *Really miss our mums…*

They all start crying and the music breaks down. The music kicks in again and they cheer, run upstage and bring out an effigy of Hook. They string it up and fire arrows at it whilst singing:

> *Nongy nangy noo noo,*
> *Shunner doobie cooking in my book,*
> *Beeeep ffffffffffppp,*

Flinger dangy blah blah,
Snoogle oogle shiny box of aaaahhhhh,
Speaking trees and houses made of chocolate.

They take the Hook effigy down and put it into a pram.

TIGER LILY appears on the platform at the back of the stage. She howls. The LOST BOYS freeze, looking up at her.

LOST BOYS: Tiger Lily!

She slides down the fireman's pole and comes into the space. THE LOST BOYS scatter.

A wolf comes in and greets her affectionately. The other wolves come in one by one until there is a group of five gathered around her.

The wolves suddenly sense that there is something wrong. They take a long slow look around. A loud thump is heard as the PIRATES try to break in through the back wall. The wolves react with a sudden move. A second and third loud thump puts them on high alert. They stand around TIGER LILY, poised to run, whimpering.

TIGER LILY: Everybody hide!

The wolves scatter.

TIGER LILY: Ready or not, here they come!

The PIRATES burst through into Neverland having smashed a hole in the wall.

The music kicks in. They step into the space as a group and hold a position in front of the hole for a moment. SMEE is with them at the back. The PIRATES begin to creep into the space carrying their weapons. They move as a group, drawn to the audience, sniffing the air as they hunt for Pan.

HOOK enters walking with a cane. She moves very slowly. The crew are all focused on her entrance. There is a teddy on the floor dropped by one of the LOST BOYS. HOOK suddenly clocks it. The PIRATES follow her gaze. She begins to move towards

it. She walks slowly and very deliberately over to the teddy.
She picks it up with her hook and holds it aloft.

HOOK: He's close. I can smell him. I can taste him.

She smells the teddy, breathing in deeply. The PIRATES mirror
her body language, breathing with her.

HOOK: Peter Pan!

She offers the teddy out towards them and they surround her.
She circles around holding the teddy up in front of them.

HOOK: If we had Peter here, now, in our grasp, what we do
with him? What would we do with him, my beautiful,
barbaric buaccaneers?

HOOK passes the teddy to SMEE who staples it to an oar. One
of the PIRATES then holds it aloft. Music. The pirate song. The
PIRATES take lead on the opening verse and HOOK comments
in the breaks.

(Crew.) Pull his little jacket off…(Hook.) Dismember with
precision and keep all the buttons.
(Crew.) Bite his little fingers off…(Hook.) Chew with care!
No noise!…(Crew.) Hush please!
(Crew.) Tear his arms and legs right off…(Hook.) Slice not
tear, I want them whole.
(Crew.) Hang him up and let him rot…(Hook.) Like a good
steak for 28 days. (Crew.) Tasty!

(Crew.) Peter…We're gonna get ya… (Hook.) Paaaan…
That's exactly what we're going to do.
(Crew.) Peter……We're gonna get ya…(Hook.) Paaaaan…
And you will be ashamed.

HOOK takes over the lead vocal in the second verse.

(Hook.) Pull out all his baby teeth… (Crew.) One by one and
very very slowly.
(Hook.) Create some pretty jewellery… (Crew.) You need a
new bracelet…(Hook.) I do.
(Hook.) Make a cut from north to south…(Crew.) You're very
partial to that method…

(Hook.) Rip all of his innards out …(Crew.) You could wear them like a scarf .(Hook.) Dainty.

(Crew.) Peter…We're gonna get ya… (Hook.) Paaaan… That's exactly what we're going to do.
(Crew.) Peter……We're gonna get ya…(Hook.) Paaaaan… And you will be ashamed.

(Crew.) Crack him like a boiled egg…(Hook.)…Ooo yes with a very soft yolk.
(Crew.) Cut the top off of his head…(Hook.)… we can hang it from the mast. (Crew.) Pretty!
(Crew.) Make his eyes into a broach…(Hook.)…Now you're talking my hearties!
(Crew.) That is Captain Hook's approach…(Hook.) …To sum up, how will it end for Pan? (Crew.) Badly.

(Crew.) Peter…We're gonna get ya (Hook.) Paaaan…That's exactly what we're going to do.
(Crew.) Peter……We're gonna get ya…(Hook.) Paaaaan… And you will be ashamed.

HOOK: You are the meanest crew of treacherous, tyrannical cutthroats that ever sailed the high seas. Show me your killing faces.

They show their scariest faces.

HOOK: What are we here for?

CREW: To get Peter Pan!

HOOK: Indeed.

She throws the torso of the teddy to the PIRATES and they go into a feeding frenzy around the teddy's body, throwing it up in the air and tearing it to pieces. SKYLIGHTS is upset about the destruction of the teddy. HOOK walks over to him.

HOOK: Skylights! What is it?

SKYLIGHTS: Nothing.

HOOK: You're sniveling. Why?

SKYLIGHTS: It's just that...

HOOK becomes a soothing mother figure.

HOOK: Come on, you can tell me.

SKYLIGHTS: Well it's just that...

HOOK: It's all going to be alright.

SKYLIGHTS: I always liked teddies. I used to have a teddy. I used to cuddle him at bedtime.

HOOK immediately kills SKYLIGHTS without mercy, all very matter of fact.

HOOK: Pirates do not have teddies. Do you all understand?

PIRATES: Yes Captain.

HOOK: Get this mess cleared up. Back to the ship and splice the main brace, if you please!

The PIRATES scatter and clear up, taking the body of the dead pirate with them only SMEE remains.

SMEE: The way you dealt with Skylights was very good, Captain.

HOOK: Snivelling over a teddy!? What kind of pirate is that?

SMEE: That's no pirate at all.

HOOK: No pirate at all. Very well put Smee. If only they all had your attention to detail.......How do I look?

SMEE: You look an absolute picture, Captain.

HOOK: A picture of what?

SMEE: A picture of menace. A picture of malice. A picture of malevolence.

HOOK slowly lifts her hook above her head.

HOOK: I have Pan to thank for this hook. I've waited a long time to shake his little hand with it. Oh I will tear him.

SMEE: And yet I have often heard you say that the hook is worth a score of hands, for combing the hair and other homely purposes.

HOOK: Ay, if I were a mother I would pray to have my children born with this instead of that.

SMEE: And it does come in very handy for killing.

HOOK: Pan sliced off my arm and flung it to a crocodile that happened to be passing by.

SMEE: Ah, your dread of the *Crocodylus Porosus*.

HOOK: Not of the species in general, Smee, but of that one particular crocodile. It liked my arm so much, that it has followed me ever since, from sea to sea and from land to land, licking its lips for the rest of me.

SMEE: In a way, it's a sort of compliment.

HOOK: I want no such compliments, Smee! I want Pan who first gave the brute its taste for me. That crocodile would have had me before this, but with my arm he swallowed my watch and it goes tick tock, so before it can reach me, I hear that tick tock and I make myself scarce.

SMEE: One day your watch will run down and your time will be up.

HOOK: Ay, that's the fear that haunts me.

HOOK collapses to her knees, the dread of the crocodile is enough to reduce her to a quivering jelly. SMEE tries to lift her out of it.

SMEE: We need a plan.

HOOK: A plan.

SMEE: Come on Captain, you're very good at plans.

HOOK: Yes, I am very good at plans.

SMEE: There's something there isn't there? Come on Captain. Unrip your plan to me!

HOOK: We'll return to the ship and bake a large cake of a jolly thickness with green sugar on it. We will leave the cake on the shore of the mermaid's lagoon. Those boys are always swimming about there, playing with the slippery mermaids. They will find the cake and they will gobble it up, because, having no mother, they don't know how dangerous it is to eat rich damp cake. And they will die.

SMEE: It is the wickedest, prettiest policy I ever heard of.

HOOK offers SMEE her hook to shake.

HOOK: Shake on't, Smee.

SMEE: May I, Captain?

SMEE touches the hook and holds it with his little finger. He sinks to his knees and she strokes his hair with the hook. HOOK begins singing the shanty as she circles SMEE.

HOOK: *Yo ho, yo ho, when I say 'claw',*
                    By fear they're overtook,
              Naught's left upon your bones when you,
                 Have shaken hands with Hook.

HOOK exits leaving SMEE on his knees.

SCENE TWO: THE WENDY BIRD

NIBS comes cautiously out of the trap, using two tin cans connected with string as a hearing device to scan the area and check if it's safe.

NIBS: Is it all clear?

SLIGHTLY: I'm checking!

One of the twins shuffles in underneath a blanket.

TWIN ONE: Well?

Slightly cycles slowly around the space on a bike.

SLIGHTLY: Yes, it's all clear.

NIBS: Definitely?

SLIGHTLY: Definitely all clear.

> *Other LOST BOYS chip in agreeing that it is all clear. They come out of their various hiding places around the stage, more confident now. After the initial relief, it becomes clear that things are rather dull when not under attack. They have no direction without PETER. They kick around the space aimlessly.*

NIBS: I wish Peter was here. He always knows what to do.

TOOTLES: I don't like it when he's away. Especially with those scary pirates so close by.

SLIGHTLY: I'm not scared of pirates. That's why Peter leaves me in charge when he's away.

NIBS: No, I'm in charge.

> *They all laugh at NIBS.*

SLIGHTLY: Don't be stupid.

> *All the LOST BOYS agree that NIBS isn't in charge.*

NIBS: Peter told me I was in charge.

TOOTLES: When?

NIBS: When no one else was looking.

TOOTLES: You're a liar.

NIBS: Am not.

TOOTLES: Yes you are.

SLIGHTLY: Alright then, if Peter left you in charge you tell us what we should do if the pirates come back.

NIBS: Ummmmm…

SLIGHTLY: Should we stand and fight or run away?

> *Suddenly NIBS sees something in the distance in the sky.*

NIBS: Hey, look at that…up there in the sky…what is it?

They are all looking up at it.

TWIN ONE: It's coming this way.

SLIGHTLY: It must be a bird.

TWIN TWO: It's very big for a bird over.

TINKER BELL *appears*.

TINKER BELL: Tootles. Chunka Tootles! *(Tootles! Big Tootles!)*

TOOTLES: Tinker Bell! Peter must be near by.

TINKER BELL *points at the object in the sky*.

TINKER BELL: Wendy cuckoo. Wendy cuckoo. Wee wee icky faultacious. Peta dee Morta! Ping ping ping! Eskud! Ping ping ping. Morta! *(Wendy bird. Wendy bird. Very dangerous. Peter says kill it! Quickly! Shoot it down!)*

TOOTLES: Peter says what?

TINKER BELL: Wendy Cuckoo. Ping ping ping! *(Wendy bird. Shoot it down!)*

TOOTLES: Boys, a message from Peter. That thing up there is a Wendy bird. Very dangerous. Peter says we must shoot it down.

The LOST BOYS encourage TOOTLES to shoot it down. They gather round him as he pulls back his bow. NIBS holds the tin cans up to his eyes like binoculars for him to look through. TOOTLES fires and there is a loud 'Ping!'. Then they watch the arrow fly before celebrating wildly as it hits WENDY.

TOOTLES: Yes!! I did it! I shot down the Wendy bird. Peter will be so pleased with me!

They watch as WENDY floats down from the sky. She flies in very slowly on a zip wire.

They sit down as she passes them and watch her all the way to the ground. SLIGHTLY and NIBS approach and examine the body.

SLIGHTLY: This is no bird.

TWIN ONE: Please confirm no beak, over.

TWIN TWO: Roger I can confirm no beak.

SLIGHTLY: I think it must be a lady.

TOOTLES: A lady?

They all follow SLIGHTLY's lead and after looking at the body agree that this is a lady.

SLIGHTLY: Tootles what have you done?

TOOTLES: I always dreamed of seeing a lady.

SLIGHTLY: A lady to look after us at last.

TOOTLES: Finally a real lady came and I have killed her.

SLIGHTLY: Peter is not going to like this.

PETER: *(From offstage.)* Cock a doodle doo!!

The LOST BOYS go into a panic. They cover WENDY with a blanket then kneel down in front of her, waiting nervously as PETER enters down the fireman's pole.

PETER: Boys, I'm back!…Why aren't you cheering?

They give a really lame cheer.

PETER: I've got great news boys! Great news! I've found us somebody who is going to tell us stories! Have you seen her? She would have come this way…

They don't know what to say. TOOTLES pushes them out of the way and shows the body to him.

TOOTLES: Here she is Peter.

PETER looks at her closely. He doesn't know how to react. He prowls around the space.

PETER: She's dead. Perhaps she is frightened of being dead. Whose arrow?

He pulls out the arrow and holds it in the air. TOOTLES steps out and puts his hand up, the others all pointing at him.

TOOTLES kneels and unbuttons his shirt, offering himself to PETER for execution.

PETER: Tootles. I'm disappointed in you.

PETER takes out his knife. He is preparing to strike when NIBS cries out.

NIBS: The lady!

PETER stops and looks. WENDY is beginning to come round, groaning. NIBS and PETER go to examine her, the other LOST BOYS look on curiously.

WENDY: Owww!! Owww!!

NIBS listens to WENDY's groans with her tin can telephone.

NIBS: I think she's saying poor Tootles.

SLIGHTLY: The Wendy lady lives.

PETER: Of course she does. The arrow struck against this. The kiss that I gave her has saved her life.

PETER gets the kiss (the acorn) out of WENDY's pocket and walks proudly away with it. The LOST BOYS follow. PETER lets them see the kiss.

SLIGHTLY: I remember kisses. Let me see that…yeah, that's a kiss alright.

NIBS: That's a lovely kiss.

TINKER BELL jumps down and tries to cast a spell on the slowly recovering WENDY.

TOOTLES: Look! Tinker Bell is angry because the Wendy lady lives. She was the one who told me to shoot her.

TINKER BELL realises she's been caught. She pretends to be trying to soothe WENDY.

TINKER BELL: La la la la la la.

PETER: Tinker Bell. You are my friend no longer. Boys, get the banishment pram!

TINKER BELL: Noooooo Peta, noooooo. I wuuu wooo Peta. *(No Peter, no. I love you Peter.)*

The LOST BOYS bring on a pram and dump TINKER BELL into it.

PETER: Tinker Bell, I never want to see you again

TINKER BELL:

> *Tinka e Peta,*
> *May na mush,*
> *Peta e Tinka,*
> *Whoosh whoosh whoosh.*

(Tinker Bell and Peter, best of friends, Peter and Tinkerbell, come on, let's go!)

Uhh wuuu oooo Peta. *(I love you Peter.)*

PETER: Alright I won't see you for a whole week then. Get her out of here boys!

TINKER BELL is wheeled away offstage. The LOST BOYS return to WENDY.

TWIN ONE: Roger roger, move the Wendy into the den over.

TOOTLES: Very very carefully.

SLIGHTLY: She'll die if she stays here.

PETER: No! You must never ever move a lady.

SLIGHTLY: She'll die then.

TOOTLES: What shall we do?

PETER: We must build her a house.

They start building the house under PETER's direction. He rides around on his bike playing his pipes. WENDY manages to get up. She staggers across the stage before collapsing again. The LOST BOYS come across to see what they can do and sing the first part of the song. WENDY's interjections in brackets.

Please stay with us and be our mum, (What?)
And read us stories one by one, (I think there's been
an awful misunderstanding.)
And wipe our tears when we cry, (I don't think
I'd be good at that.)
Please sing to us a lullaby.

Oh Please... (Peter.)
Wendy,
Oh please...
Wendy...

**The song is interrupted when JOHN and MICHAEL come in.
MICHAEL bouncing happily.**

JOHN: Hello Wendy, hello Peter.

**PETER goes into defensive mode. He has forgotten who they
are and thinks the newcomers might be hostile. He holds his
knife out at them and the other LOST BOYS follow suit.**

PETER: Stand back. Who are you?

JOHN: I'm John. Remember?

PETER: Who's the other one?

MICHAEL: I'm Michael. We flew out of the window together.

**PETER remembers them and everyone relaxes again. The LOST
BOYS greet the new arrivals, welcoming them in.**

PETER: Hello John. Hello Michael. We're building a house for
Wendy.

JOHN: Why? She's only a girl.

PETER: What did you say?

JOHN: I said she's only a girl.

PETER: Snake bite!

PETER twists his arm as punishment.

PETER: Never speak about a girl like that again. Come on, we
need to get the roof on.

The doors and the roof go on the house. Tyres are used to make a seat for WENDY. She makes her way to it unsteadily and sits.

CURLY: Yes! Now we can play mummies and daddies!

They all cheer 'Yes!' excited about the new game.

PETER: Mummies and daddies! I'm daddy.

ALL: Presents!

The LOST BOYS line up outside the house with their gifts.

Once they have given their presents they go and sit in the house together.

PETER: Hello Mother.

WENDY: Hello Father.

The Twins knock on the door.

PETER: Oh Mother, there is somebody at the door.

WENDY: Come in.

TWIN ONE: Come in come in mother goose over.

TWIN TWO: Come in, moonbase calling.

WENDY: Hello

TWINS: We are the twins. over

The TWINS give her their walkie talkies.

WENDY: Thank you.

WENDY isn't sure what they are. She puts them down next to her seat and the twins immediately pick them back up again. MICHAEL is next. His gift is a can of engine oil.

MICHAEL: Hello Mother. Wendy, we're playing mummies and daddies. I brought you this oil. To make your bath smell nice.

WENDY: Mmmm, lavender, my favourite.

NIBS has brought the tin can phone.

NIBS: Hello Mother. My name is Nibs and this is my favourite telephone. *(Into the phone.)* Hello Mother, can you hear me?

WENDY: *(Into the phone.)* Loud and clear thanks!

NIBS makes a 'call me' sign to WENDY as she goes to sit with the others.

CURLY brings a battered old telephone directory.

CURLY: Hello Mother I'm actually Curly and I've brought you this story book so you can read to us you're welcome.

WENDY: Oh I love thrillers.

JOHN comes in. He is very sulky.

JOHN: Hello Wendy.

PETER: Get out John!

JOHN goes back out.

PETER: Play the game John.

JOHN: I am playing the game Peter.

PETER: Snake bite!

JOHN: Alright, I'll play the game.

He enters again.

JOHN: Hello Mother.

WENDY: I didn't say come in yet.

JOHN: Oh come on Wendy!

He goes out and knocks on the door

WENDY: Come in.

JOHN: Hello Mother, I got you a gun.

PETER likes the gun. He takes it from WENDY. She chases after him all the way round the house and eventually grabs it back from him.

WENDY: That's my present.

TOOTLES knocks and enters.

WENDY: Come in.

TOOTLES: Hello my name's Tootles.

WENDY: Hello Tootles. What have you brought me?

TOOTLES just gives WENDY a big hug. The LOST BOYS surround her all trying to hug her. They continue with the song. WENDY's spoken interventions in brackets.

Please stay with us and be our mum,
And read us stories one by one, (stop looking at me like that.)
And wipe our tears when we cry, (I'm trying to tell you.)
Please sing to us a lullaby. (Ooooooh noooooo.)

> *Oh Please…Wendy*
> *Oh please…Wendy*

Finally WENDY has had enough.

WENDY: Stop! Stop it! Please can you stop singing? I can't be your mother.

TOOTLES immediately bursts into tears.

TOOTLES: I just wanted you to be our mother and now you're saying that you can't and it's not fair…

He dissolves into inaudible sobs and the other LOST BOYS follow suit.

WENDY: Would you please all just stop crying! I cannot be your mother. But if you stop crying and you promise to call me by my proper name then I will tell you a story.

They are all elated.

ALL: Yay! Mother!

They go into the house and snuggle down. PETER closes the front doors, remaining outside on guard.

PETER: Goodnight children.

TWIN ONE: Goodnight Father.

TWIN TWO: Goodnight rubber duck. Over and out.

SCENE THREE: TIGER LILY

PETER senses that someone is coming. He hides behind the house.

TIGER LILY enters. She sees the house and is appalled.

TIGER LILY: What is this piece of junk doing here? Who's
done this? Let me take a wild guess…

> *TIGER LILY howls and the wolves enter. They gather at the
> front of the house as TIGER LILY sings.*

> *Some little boy's been sneaking round my place,*
> *He's got a cheek showing his pretty face.*

> *Some little kid been creeping round my patch,*
> *Better get ready there's gonna be a death match.*

> *Some little lad crossed over my line,*
> *He's gonna get hit pretty good this time.*

> *Some little boy been standing on my spot,*
> *He's gonna pay gonna pay gonna pay a lot.*

> *Peter I can see you, there's nowhere you can fly to.*

> *PETER shows himself.*

PETER: I'm not flying anywhere Tiger Lily.

TIGER LILY: There you are you stupid boy. What is this?

PETER: It's a house. I built it for my new friend Wendy.

TIGER LILY: It's rubbish. I'm going to smash it down.

PETER: You'll have to smash me down first.

> *TIGER LILY comes down from the house.*

TIGER LILY: You want to take me on?

PETER: Dare you to a death match!

TIGER LILY: I accept your challenge!

> *The music kicks in.*

> *They draw swords. The wolves are behind TIGER LILY.*

They square up to each other. Swiping their swords through the air, testing the blades.

They swordfight with their imaginary swords.

PETER catches himself in the eye with his.

A wolf grabs PETER's sword and he struggles to get it back.

He takes a bow and arrow instead, fires it and TIGER LILY catches it between her teeth.

They swordfight, then PETER scares the wolves when they try to approach him.

They draw light sabers and battle with those in slow motion. TIGER LILY loses hers and has to roll out of the way to escape PETER.

PETER: Give me a beat!

The fight turns into a dance off. PETER does some bad breakdance and TIGER LILY responds.

PETER: Come on everyone!

The wolves join in. PETER does the worm and everyone starts dancing together freestyle.

WENDY appears on the house looking over the top. She clambers on to the top of the ladder. The music ends and they all howl.

WENDY fires some mime arrows. The others all stare at her in confusion.

PETER: What are you doing Wendy?

WENDY: I'm hunting squirrel to feed the Lost Boys Peter. Peow. Peow.

TIGER LILY: Who's this?

WENDY climbs down from the house. The wolves sniff her. TIGER LILY and WENDY suss each other out.

WENDY: I am Wendy Darling.

TIGER LILY: I'm Tiger Lily.

TIGER LILY tickles WENDY and they both fall down laughing.

TIGER LILY: You should come and play with us some time!

TIGER LILY and the wolves run off howling.

WENDY: Can we play with her Peter? Can we play?

PETER: Alright. Come on then! Let's have an adventure!

PETER sets off running. WENDY follows him.

The whole company begin running in a circle.

SCENE FOUR: NEVERLAND BECOMES NORMAL

'Another adventure another adventure another adventure another adventure' echoes on the soundtrack. All the Neverland characters and the Darling children stand in a line at the back of the stage. They move forward very very slowly as a voiceover plays on the soundtrack, detailing the adventures they have been on over the time.

PETER: Buried treasure at Moonlight cove.

Butter bean butter bean where are you?

Chain tag limbo.

WENDY: The defiance of the lions.

MICHAEL: Ghost in the court of the King of Milan.

JOHN: Continuous cricket.

MICHAEL: High flying kites.

PETER: A brush with death at the Grizzly Gulch

WENDY: Question one: What colour were Mother's eyes?

JOHN: Her eyes were blue.

MICHAEL: Her eyes were green.

PETER: Here comes the butcher all dressed in blue

JOHN: Brown.

MICHAEL: Purple.

WENDY: Question two: Describe Mother's party dress.

PETER: Lost and alone in the Ata-vada desert.

JOHN: A long flowing ball gown.

MICHAEL: With glass slippers.

JOHN: At midnight she wore rags.

PETER: The navigation of the burning maze.

WENDY: Question three: How long ago did we leave?

MICHAEL: Not so long.

JOHN: But how long ago?

PETER: The mangled blade. Sharks and minnows. Jump the volcano. The dark streets of London. The rescue of Tiger Lily!

Act Three: The Mermaid's Lagoon

SCENE ONE: RESCUE MISSION

We snap from the time passing sequence back into present time.

PETER: Tiger Lily has been captured by the pirates Wendy! Would you like to rescue her?

WENDY: Have they taken her to Marooner's Rock?

PETER: I fear they have.

WENDY: But the lagoon is dangerous for mortals at the turn at the moon. And besides Peter you know I have strict rules about being in bed by seven.

PETER: But Wendy she will drown when the tide rises for then the rock is submerged.

WENDY: We must cast our lives to fate Peter. For Tiger Lily is our friend.

PETER: We must. But I am Captain, follow my instructions at all times. Let me stay up front. And stay very, very quiet when I tell you to.

PETER: Ay ay Captain.

They start to play the game of the rescue of TIGER LILY.

PETER: Ready? Let's go.

Music begins. They start running.

WENDY: How many adventures have you had Peter?

PETER: More than you can count.

WENDY: How old are you Peter?

PETER: I'm not sure. Quite young. I ran away the day I was born. I ran away and I never went back.

JOHN and MICHAEL appear and start following them.

JOHN: Hello Wendy, hello Peter.

MICHAEL: Wait for me! Why are we running?

PETER: We're on a rescue mission!

WENDY: It's going to be very dangerous.

JOHN: Great!

PETER: It's not a joke John.

MICHAEL: Who are we going to rescue?

WENDY: Tiger Lily. The pirates are going to drown her at Marooner's Rock.

PETER: We need to get there before sundown and it's a long way, so get a move on.

They now start to encounter dangers on their journey.

PETER: Watch out for the biting spiders.

They all jump around as if the floor is covered in spiders.

JOHN: A pterodactyl!

The pterodactyl dive bombs them.

WENDY: A purple lung crushing snake!

The lung crushing snake crushes them, but then PETER pops it with a pin and it deflates.

MICHAEL: A giant slug!

JOHN: It's all slimy! Let's wash it off at the waterfall!

They edge their way along the front of the stage as if shuffling along a narrow ledge on the side of a mountain. Eventually they reach their destination. They stop and crouch down at the front of the stage, mesmerized by the beauty of the Mermaid's Lagoon.

WENDY: Look, over there.

MICHAEL: What are they?

JOHN: Bobbing in the water.

WENDY: Mermaids…

PETER: Follow me!

They exit.

SCENE TWO: MERMAID'S LAGOON

The MERMAIDS enter. Some of them swing leisurely on swings, some lounge on Marooner's Rock, doing their make-up or brushing their hair. Music plays and they sing, flirting outrageously with the audience.

Hello boys please come and play,
Hello boys just for one day,
We'll make you smile,
Maybe you'll just learn to like it.

Coo eee boys won't you come in?
Coo eee boys look at my fin,
Just for a while we'll make you smile.

I could pretend to be your mummy,
I'll brush your hair and stroke your tummy.
Why won't you, why don't you stay?

Oooo Oooo Oooooo,
Ooo Ooo Ooo Ooooo,
Oooo Oooo Oooooo,
Ooo Ooo Ooo Ooooo.

PETER, WENDY, MICHAEL and JOHN climb on to the rock. They are astonished by what they see.

JOHN: Real Mermaids!

WENDY: Oh, they are the most beautiful things I have ever seen

MICHAEL: I wish we could play with them.

The MERMAIDS have noticed PETER and the children. They all swim around, trying to be the closest to PETER.

MERMAID 1: Oooo look, it's Peter.

MERMAID 2: Hi Peter.

MERMAID 3: Hiya.

PETER: Evening Mermaids.

They all laugh as if he has said something really funny.

MERMAID 4: Haven't seen you for a while.

MERMAID 5: Where you been Peter?

MERMAID 1: He's been all over.

MERMAID 3: You get around, don't you Peter?

PETER: I don't have time to tell you now. It's a very long tale.

They all laugh at PETER's joke.

MERMAID 2: You are so funny Peter.

MERMAID 4: Who are your friends Peter? Are you coming in for a swim? The water's lovely.

JOHN: I will.

PETER: Be careful John.

The MERMAIDS lure JOHN into the water and start tickling him. At first it's fun but then it begins to get unpleasant. The mermaids force his head under the water. PETER blows his pipe sharply to frighten them off. JOHN staggers back on to the rock.

JOHN: What happened?

PETER: Mermaids are very beautiful but very cruel creatures. They like to pull boys and girls like you into the water to drown them.

JOHN: Let's go home.

PETER: I did warn you that this was a dangerous place.

The sound of a fog horn on a tiny boat.

PETER: Fly!

PETER and the children scatter away from the rock. SMEE and STARKEY enter on a little boat with TIGER LILY as their captive. She is bound, gagged and tied to a stake. SMEE is singing a version of HOOK's shanty.

SMEE:

> *Yo ho yo ho five fathoms deep,*
> *A thousand lives below,*
> *Soul's breath from lungs untimely ripped,*
> *Cold coral eyes aglow.*

The boat circles the rock. WENDY howls in an attempt to reassure TIGER LILY.

SMEE: Looks like the dogs will go hungry tonight Tiger Lily.

> *Yo ho yo ho the tide doth rise,*
> *Cold bodies lie beneath,*
> *Flesh and blood from bones removed,*
> *By a thousand fishes teeth.*

SMEE and STARKEY arrive at the rock.

STARKEY: Let's get her on the rock quickly and get out of here.

SMEE: Why the hurry Starkey? I always rather liked it here. The morbid atmosphere. The stench of death.

They put TIGER LILY on the rock, tying her to another stake.

STARKEY: The spirits of dead sailors haunts this place. Everyone knows that.

SMEE: They do Starkey, they do. I sometimes think you can feel their little fingers clutching at your ankles as you dangle your feet in the water.

STARKEY: Let's get back to the ship this place gives me the willies.

SMEE: I enjoyed our little chats Tiger Lily, but I fear this will be our last.

TIGER LILY tries to speak through her gag.

SMEE: What? I didn't quite catch that?

She tries again.

SMEE: Did you want to say something? It's not getting through. This is what happens to people who get caught prowling around on our ship. Soon you will be food for the fishes.

The PIRATES hear WENDY calling to PETER.

WENDY: Do something Peter!

STARKEY: What's that?

They both listen for the voice. PETER covers the call by crying out from the mist, impersonating HOOK.

PETER: *(As Hook.)* Ahoy there you lubbers!

SMEE: It's the Captain. She must be swimming out to us.

STARKEY: Captain? What does the Captain want?

SMEE: We have done exactly as you commanded Captain. Tiger Lily is tied fast to the rock.

PETER: *(As Hook.)* Set her free.

SMEE: Set her free Captain? …But if we…

PETER: *(As Hook.)* Cut her bonds or I'll plunge my hook in you!

STARKEY: Yes Captain.

SMEE: Quickly Starkey. Do as the Captain orders!

STARKEY climbs back on to the rock to release TIGER LILY. STARKEY is wary of her. Once the ropes are off she hits STARKEY, who falls. TIGER LILY kicks STARKEY off the rock, removes her gag and blows a kiss to SMEE before jumping off the back of the rock. All the children howl in celebration.

There is a loud clang and HOOK suddenly appears from behind the rock completely breathless. She struggles on to the rock with the help of the PIRATES.

SMEE: What is it Captain?

HOOK: Those boys have found…they have found…they have found a mother!

60

SMEE and STARKEY register that this is serious.

SMEE: A mother?

STARKEY: They found a mother.

SMEE: They found a mother!?

STARKEY: What is a mother Captain?

HOOK has to think hard about how to describe a mother.

HOOK: Do'st not know Starkey? A mother is…A mother is…A mother…

The Neverbird flies in and sits on the eggs in her nest, which is floating around the lagoon. HOOK points it out.

HOOK: There is a lesson in mothers for you. The nest must have fallen in the water, but would that bird desert her eggs?

The Neverbird nest drifts away.

HOOK: O evil day. If Peter Pan has found a mother then how will I ever get to him. If Peter Pan has found a mother then why would he ever want me? Nobody wants me!

PETER calls out from the fog imitating HOOK's voice. Everyone joins in so that the call echoes around the lagoon.

PETER: *(As voice.)* Nobody wants me.

WENDY: Nobody wants me.

MICHAEL: Nobody wants me.

JOHN: Nobody wants me.

HOOK and the PIRATES are fearful about the echo. They look around them unsure where the voice is coming from.

HOOK: The lagoon has a very particular echo tonight. Why do you taunt me echo?

PETER: *(As voice.)* Because you are a codfish.

HOOK: A codfish?

The word 'codfish' echoes around the lagoon to TIGER LILY.

TIGER LILY: A codfish that's going to get battered when I get my hands on you!

They all howl. HOOK realises that TIGER LILY is free.

HOOK: Tiger Lily. Where is she boys?

SMEE: We let her go.

HOOK: Let her go?

STARKEY: 'Twas your orders Captain. You called out to us to let her go.

HOOK: Brimstone and gall, what cozening is here? I gave no such order. Spirit that haunts this dark lagoon tonight, who are you?

PETER: I am your echo.

HOOK: Have you another name?

PETER: Yes.

HOOK: Vegetable?

PETER: No.

HOOK: Mineral?

PETER: No.

HOOK: Animal?

PETER: Yes.

HOOK: Man?

PETER: No!

HOOK: Boy?

PETER: Yes.

HOOK: Ordinary boy?

WENDY: Certainly not!

HOOK: Wonderful boy?

PETER: Yes! Can't you guess?

HOOK: No I couldn't possibly.

PETER: It's me! Peter Pan.

HOOK: Now we have him! Into the water, Smee, Starkey, take him dead or alive.

PETER: Lam into those pirates!

WENDY, TIGER LILY, JOHN and MICHAEL launch the first attack on SMEE and STARKEY. There is a fight in the water. STARKEY swims away in terror pursued by the children.

WENDY circles the rock, pulling at HOOK's leg. HOOK tries to shake her off, but WENDY clings on and eventually HOOK falls down the side of the rock. PETER climbs on to the rock to attack. HOOK flails at him, but it is easy for PETER to avoid the blows as he has the high ground. HOOK collapses back, exhausted.

PETER: My turn!

He swipes his knife at HOOK and advances, HOOK retreats. PETER towers over her.

PETER: Come on!

PETER relaxes, this is too easy.

PETER: This is hardly a fair fight now, is it?

He offers his hand to pull HOOK back on to the rock and even things up. HOOK takes his hand and bites it, which is both painful and shocking to PETER.

PETER: Ahhhh!

HOOK climbs back on the rock and is about to strike PETER who is still distracted by the pain from the bite. Suddenly she hears the 'tick tock' of the crocodile. She looks around terrified and as she does so swings her hook and wounds PETER in the chest. He collapses.

The crocodile chases HOOK offstage.

WENDY: Michael, John, scramble up the rocks and get out of here.

JOHN: What about you Wendy?

WENDY: I'm going to stay with Peter.

JOHN and MICHAEL exit.

WENDY: Peter, we must get back to shore.

PETER: Yes.

WENDY: Shall we swim or fly?

PETER: Do you think you could swim or fly to the island Wendy, without my help?

WENDY: No. I am too tired.

PETER: I am wounded.

WENDY: Peter.

WENDY reaches for him to look at the wound. PETER flinches.

WENDY: The water is rising.

PETER: Yes.

WENDY: We shall both be drowned.

The kite flies in.

PETER: Look. There's a kite.

WENDY: That could carry both of us home.

PETER: It would not be strong enough to carry both of us.

PETER grabs the tale of the kite.

WENDY: Then you should go, you are wounded.

PETER is already fastening WENDY to the kite.

PETER: No Wendy. You must go.

PETER eases WENDY off the edge of the rock and she flies off with the kite.

WENDY: Peter! I won't go without you. Peter!

PETER: You'll be safe Wendy. Hold on tight.

WENDY: Peter! Peter!

PETER: Don't let go and don't look down. Goodbye Wendy.

> *WENDY exits. As she does so the ensemble unfurl their streamers which will become the waters rising around the rock. PETER alone on the rock as the waters rise.*

PETER: He was alone now. Soon the rock would be submerged. Pale rays of light tiptoed across the waters. And by and by he heard the most melancholy sound in the world. The mermaids calling to the moon. Peter was not quite like other boys, but he was afraid at last. A tremor ran through him, like a shudder passing over the sea. But on the sea one shudder follows another till there are hundreds of them, and Peter felt just one. Next moment he was standing tall on the rock again with that smile on his face and a drum beating inside of him. and it was saying; and it was saying; To die will be an awfully big adventure.

> *Black out.*

INTERVAL.

Act Four: The Home Under the Ground

SCENE ONE: HOOK

Music. HOOK stands up and begins a very slow walk towards the front of the stage. She is out of her costume, has removed her wig and is completely bald. She looks small and vulnerable, nothing like the fearsome Captain we have seen in the first half. She sings. During the course of the song SMEE ministers to her and helps her slowly get back into her costume, transforming herself through the song back into her public HOOK persona.

Where did the time go?
What have I become?
Too many moons, scorched by the sun

Once I was youthful,
I too had wings,
All that I wanted were childlike things.

Peter…Peter

The hands spin like scythes,
The face laughs and leers,
I'm drowning in seconds and minutes and years.

Shadows they clothe me,
Like parchment my skin,
All your subtractions tattooed within.

Peter…Peter

Now I am hollow,
Broken with badness,
Now I am darkness twisted with sadness.

I am brutality,
I am battered,
I am blood,
And I will break you.

Peter…Peter

Anchors and serpents,
I will wrap around your ankles,
And your milk teeth,
I'll make into jewels,
You'll adorn me,
I'll pierce your sweet body,
Like a fish on my hook,
And you'll hang like a worm,
And it won't be a game,
That will end,
You will know that,
There's no more pretend,
When your heart breaks like mine.

(Hook.)
You fed me,
To creatures,
I was your,
Playtime,
You'll never,
Escape me,
Pan..Pan…Pan…Pan…Pan.

(Pan.)
Oh the cleverness of me,
Fly with me and you'll be free,
Don't need a mother or a dad,
Oh I am such a cocky lad,
I am youth and I am joy,
And I will always be,
a boy..boy..boy..boy..boy.

By the end of the song HOOK is fully dressed.

HOOK: Find their den, Smee! I will not rest until I have hunted them down and I have them in my clutches.

SMEE co-ordinates the search for the den, turning his hat into a listening device. Sonar pings are heard on the soundtrack. At the last moment he hears something of interest.

SMEE: Excellent. The Captain will be pleased.

SCENE TWO: THE HOME UNDER THE GROUND

The LOST BOYS, WENDY, MICHAEL and JOHN are all in the underground den. WENDY is telling them one of their favourite stories, the tale of how PETER escaped from Marooner's Rock. The rock is made out of some crates covered with a cloth. WENDY puppeteers a teddy as PETER. The LOST BOYS join in by making the different things that come into the story

WENDY: The waves were crashing against Marooner's Rock. The wound in Father's chest was gushing with blood and he was growing as pale as death. But he wasn't afraid.

ALL: To die would be an awfully big adventure.

WENDY: The black waters of the lagoon were rising slowly to his neck. Dark, blubbery creatures were slithing up from the fathomless depths, circling the rock ready to devour Peter, snapping at his toes. It was then good fortune made her intervention. A magnificent Neverbird!

LOST BOYS: A Neverbird!

WENDY: Her nest had fallen into the waves but she heard Peter's desperate cries:

MICHAEL joins in and plays PETER.

MICHAEL: Save me, save me!

NIBS uses a watering can to be the Neverbird. Another LOST BOY carries an upturned umbrella as the nest.

WENDY: She steered against the tide, her tail moving as a rudder, and moored her nest against the rock. She called out to Peter:

NIBS: 'Get in Peter, the water's rising.'

WENDY: Peter was too weak so she shook her beak at him and cried:

Nibs: 'Peter! Get in the nest or you'll drown!'

The teddy bear PETER jumps into the nest and sails away from the rock.

WENDY: With his last trace of strength Peter threw himself from the rock and into her warm comfortable nest. And they drifted on the waves and circled the lagoon for a night and a day...until at last they washed back on to the shore, where Peter, gasping, hauled himself up onto the rocks and crawled all the way back across the island, into the loving bosom of his family, where, safe at last, he cried-

From off stage there is a mighty blast on the horn.

ALL: Father...

Everyone immediately lines up ready to greet PETER on his return. PETER rumbles down the chute and rolls into the space.

PETER: Cock a doodle doo!

ALL: Oh the cleverness of you!

WENDY and PETER go into the 'mother and father' game.

WENDY: Hello Father.

PETER: Oh I love this game. Hello Mother. How have the children been today?

WENDY: They've been exceptionally naughty as ever dear.

PETER inspects the line of children.

WENDY: Did you have a terribly difficult day at the office, Father?

PETER: Oh it was a terribly difficult day Mother. I was out hunting with the Twins.

WENDY: Did you catch anything?

PETER picks up a space hopper.

PETER: I caught an orange Smashy-Liffy-Doctipus, so I ripped it's head off and brought it home as a trophy!

The children cheer.

TWINS: *(Offstage.)* Incoming. Incoming. Permission to land? Over.

ALL: Permission granted.

The twins rumble down the chute into the den.

TWIN ONE: What's for tea Mother?

TWIN TWO: We're starving, over.

SLIGHTLY: Yes I'm really hungry

CURLY: I'm actually famished

They surround WENDY demanding to be fed.

WENDY: Alright! Let me take your orders please. Make your way to the table.

On an imaginary notebook she records their orders as they make their way to an imaginary table.

CURLY: Fish finger sandwiches with hundreds and thousands actually.

TWIN ONE: A creamy chicken thing.

TWIN TWO: With jelly babies, over.

NIBS: Ice cream on toast.

MICHAEL: Pasta with bananas.

SLIGHTLY: Sausages and jam.

A series of other suggestions follows

'Baked beans and chocolate fingers!'
'Vanilla fudge korma!'
'Bacon with toffees!'
'Potato smiley faces!'
'Mud pattie!'

TOOTLES: A nice piece of fruit from the fruit bowl?

They all stop and look at him.

TOOTLES: Which has been used to create a delicious banoffee pie.

WENDY: Right, sit up nicely. Put your napkins on, elbows off the table and tuck in.

They start eating in the most ill-mannered way possible.

> *Fish finger sandwiches, fish finger sandwiches,*
> *Fish finger sandwiches, fish finger sandwiches,*
> *Oooooo yummy yummy yummy yummy,*
> *With cheese.*

CURLY: My compliments to the chef!

> *Creamy chicken thing, creamy chicken thing,*
> *Creamy chicken thing, creamy chicken thing,*
> *Oooooooo with mushrooms too.*

> *Roast beef and ketchup,*
> *Jam and ham sandwiches,*
> *Chips and marmalade,*
> *Custard freshly made,*
> *Fizzy pop and spotted dick.*

PETER: Mother I think the children should be eating healthy nutritious food so they grow up big and strong. Maybe something pink...like...

> *Taramasalata Taramasalata,*
> *Taramasalata Taramasalata,*
> *Oooooo yummy yummy yummy yummy,*
> *With cucumber.*

> *Crispy curly kale Crispy curly kale,*
> *Crispy curly kale Crispy curly kale,*
> *Ooo With bean sprouts too.*

> *Quinoa protein bar,*
> *Gluten free pastry,*
> *Vegan carob slice,*
> *Mung beans peas and rice,*
> *Carrot juice and hummus dip.*

PETER: Father I'm sorry to say that the children become disgracefully insubordinate unless they are allowed to eat exactly what they want, so I am going to have to insist that a high carbohydrate, high sugar diet is reinstated with immediate effect.

> *Pancake lemon pie Pancake lemon pie,*
> *Pancake lemon pie Pancake lemon pie,*
> *Oooooo yummy yummy yummy yummy,*
> *With crisps.*

> *Gooey chocolate muffin Gooey chocolate muffin,*
> *Gooey chocolate muffin Gooey chocolate muffin,*
> *Ooo with gravy too.*

> *Hot dogs and strudels,*
> *Jelly and noodles,*
> *Toffee pizza cake,*
> *Chocolate burger bake,*
> *Cheesy puff and jammy dodger.*

The song stops abruptly.

CURLY: John actually just spat in my food!

JOHN: Curly didn't eat his ice cream. Actually!

NIBS: Father stole my fish finger!

TOOTLES: It was my fish finger in the first place!

MICHAEL: No he took it from me.

They all start arguing with each other. WENDY blows the horn to make them quiet.

WENDY: If you've all finished then you may be excused from the table and sit nicely by the fire until bed time.

The LOST BOYS settle down around the fireplace.

WENDY: All the family together, isn't it wonderful?

PETER: Oh yes Mother, look at all the children. Pretty as a picture. We should take a photograph! I'll set the camera up. Ready? 5, 4, 3, 2, 1. Cheese!

Camera flash goes off.

PETER: I love cosy nights… Hang on a minute, its not a cosy night! What night is it?

ALL: It's Saturday night.

PETER: Saturday night is dancing night!

The LOST BOYS do some freestyle dancing as the band sings.

BAND:

> *Ooooooo,*
> *Saturday night,*
> *Saturday night.*

BAND: And that was "Saturday Night" by Wet Denim. Now we're gonna slow things down a bit. Here's one for all you lovers out there.

The band begin playing the introduction to 'Close to you' by The Carpenters. The LOST BOYS plead with WENDY and PETER to dance.

NIBS: Father, why don't you dance with Mother?

PETER: No, I have to read newspapers.

CURLY: Mother I'm sure you'd like to dance?

WENDY: No, I haven't got the right knickers on.

WENDY moves towards PETER.

WENDY: Well I suppose we could give it try?

PETER: I suppose we could.

WENDY: But only if you want to…

PETER: I will if you will.

WENDY: I will if you will.

PETER: And you will if I will if you will.

NIBS: Get on with it!

The LOST BOYS have settled back into the skips to watch. PETER makes an elaborate bow as he did when he first met WENDY. WENDY reciprocates. The LOST BOYS play 'Close to You' by the Carpenters, all joining in with the singing and playing instruments along with the band.

At first PETER and WENDY dance awkwardly together on the carpet. Half way through the song they take off and fly together.

When the song comes to an end they return to the ground where they bow to one another.

PETER: I haven't danced like that in sixty-two years.

WENDY: Not bad for a couple of old timers.

PETER: I must rest my weary old bones by the fire.

PETER lies down on the rug. WENDY comes to sit next to him.

WENDY: Father, I know that after the children I'm not quite as springy as I used to be and I may be in some ways a little past my best, but you wouldn't want to change me would you?

PETER: Oh no darling. Are we still playing the game, Wendy?

WENDY: Sort of a game Peter.

PETER: It's only pretend.

WENDY: But they really are our children, Peter, yours and mine.

PETER: They're not my children. I'm not their father. You're not their mother. If I was their father I would have to be very old. I don't ever want to be old. I want always to be a little boy and to have fun. Play the game Wendy.

WENDY: Peter, what are your true feelings for me?

PETER: Tiger Lily does this. And Tinker Bell. Just when we're having the best fun.

WENDY: And I don't suppose you have any idea why, do you?

PETER: Perhaps they want to be my mother.

WENDY: No they don't want to be your mother you silly boy.

PETER: What is it that they want?

WENDY: There's no point explaining. You just wouldn't understand. Come on everyone, wake up! Let's have a story.

NIBS: Which story shall we have Mother?

WENDY: I think we should have your favourite story.

PETER: I hate that story.

WENDY: You can just cover your ears then, like you usually do.

PETER groans and slumps down on the tyres while the LOST BOYS gather around WENDY.

WENDY: There was once a very nice lady…

SLIGHTLY: There is a lady in the story.

TOOTLES: She isn't dead is she?

WENDY: Oh no.

TOOTLES: I am glad to hear that. Are you glad Michael?

MICHAEL: I am awfully glad.

WENDY: There was also a very nice gentleman. The gentleman's name was Mr Darling and the lady was called Mrs Darling.

JOHN: I think I've heard of them

WENDY: They were married and what do you think they had?

NIBS: A white rat?

WENDY: They had three children and a faithful nurse called Nana. One night Mr Darling was very angry and he chained Nana up in the yard, and all the children flew away out of the bedroom window, past the moon and the stars till they arrived in a magical world where they met the Lost Boys.

TOOTLES: Was one of them called Tootles?

WENDY: Yes he was.

TOOTLES: I'm in the story. Nibs, I am in the story.

NIBS: Can I be in the story too?

WENDY: You are all in the story. The children lived with the Lost Boys for many many moons. They had such a lovely time. But think. Think for a moment about the poor unhappy parents.

LOST BOYS: Oooo.

WENDY: Left at home with the empty beds!

LOST BOYS: Oooo.

WENDY: Their hearts broken.

TWIN ONE: It's a very sad story.

TWIN TWO: I don't see how it can have a happy ending, do you Curly?

CURLY: I'm actually feeling very anxious.

WENDY: If you knew how great was a mother's love then you wouldn't feel anxious.

SLIGHTLY: I do like a mother's love.

> *All the other LOST BOYS agree that a mother's love is great. PETER groans again.*

WENDY: One night the children flew back to their old house. The window was open, and they threw their arms around the huddled figures and their parents leapt with joy, and they danced and laughed and ate chocolate pudding until they were sick. And they all lived happily ever after.

> *PETER is now in real agony.*

WENDY: Is something the matter Peter?

PETER: You are wrong about mothers Wendy. I had a mother once. I had a cosy bed and a nice soft blanket. The window was open and I just went for a little fly, I was flying in the sky with the birds and the clouds. But when I wanted to go back to my little bed and my little blanket, the window was shut. And barred. And there was another little boy sleeping in my bed. Mothers do not keep the window open.

WENDY: Yes they do.

PETER: You are wrong about mothers.

MICHAEL: Wendy, I want to go home.

JOHN: I want to go home too.

WENDY: Yes, collect your things, we're going home.

The LOST BOYS plead with her not to go.

CURLY: You can't leave Mother, we actually need you.

TWIN ONE: Don't leave us Mother.

TWIN TWO: Please. Over.

SLIGHTLY: You can't go.

NIBS: We won't let you.

SLIGHTLY: We'll tie you up.

CURLY: Let's tie her up, then she won't be able to go.

They have surrounded her. TOOTLES intervenes on her behalf.

TOOTLES: Leave her alone. All of you! If she wants to go then she can do. Any of you that try to stop her...I'll kill you. Understand?

The other LOST BOYS back down.

WENDY: Thank you Tootles. That was very brave. Now look everyone, if any of you would like to come with us I feel sure I can get my parents to adopt you all.

NIBS: Won't we be rather a handful?

WENDY: No of course not. You may not all get a bed but you will all have your own pillow.

MICHAEL: Nibs and Curly can sleep in our bed.

JOHN: Everyone can share my blanket.

SLIGHTLY: Peter, shall we go?

PETER: Alright. Twins, find Tiger Lily she'll guide you to the edge of the island and then Tinker Bell can show you the way back to the mainland.

The TWINS exit.

WENDY: Now gather anything you wish to bring with you… small things.

They gather up their things.

WENDY: Right, you must all take your medicine before we leave

They all drink from their medicine bottles.

ALL: Eeurgh!

WENDY: Peter. Get your things.

PETER: I'm not coming.

WENDY: We will find your mother.

PETER: No.

WENDY: Peter isn't coming.

PETER: If you find your mothers, I hope you like them.

WENDY: In that case I must advise you never to go without a boiled egg in the morning, change your flannel on a regular basis, and make sure you take your medicine every day.

PETER blows his horn and they all cheer. As they leave they are full of questions for JOHN and MICHAEL about what it will be like. They have almost forgotten PETER PAN.

WENDY: Goodbye Peter.

SCENE THREE: PETER'S NIGHTMARE

Everyone leaves and PETER is alone. He starts playing to try and comfort himself, but he can't get into it. As the music starts he begins building a nest for himself, filling his pram with blankets. He gets in, but when he does he is overtaken by a dream, he is flying, falling, barred from the window.

> Suddenly I'm feeling older,
> Suddenly life is much colder,

I didn't choose so how could I lose,
Lose, lose, lose, lose, lose, lose…

Oh… Peter… hear my cry…
Oh… Peter… hear my cry…

Suddenly I'm feeling older,
Suddenly Neverland is colder,
How did I lose this game I didn't choose.
Choose, choose, choose, choose…

Oh… Peter… hear my cry…
Oh… Peter… hear my cry…
Oh… Peter… hear my cry…
Oh… Peter… hear my cry…

Oh please, Wendy…
It's not too late…
Oh please, Oh Wendy…

I wish that you were here,
Wish you were always near,
I wish that you would stay,
Be near me every day.

Oh please, Wendy…
It's not too late…
Oh please, Oh Wendy…
Oh please, Oh, Wendy…
Oh please, Oh, Wendy…
Oh please, Oh, Wendy…
Oh please, Oh, Wendy…

At the end of the song, PETER is asleep in the pram.

SCENE FOUR: TINKER BELL POISONED

HOOK orders the PIRATES to get the LOST BOYS.

HOOK: Smee. Get them!

The LOST BOYS all twist their arms up behind themselves as if captured.

SMEE: I'm sorry we haven't been properly introduced. My name is Smee. Delighted to make your acquaintance.

WENDY: I'm sorry I can't return the compliment.

SMEE: How unkind! You've hurt my feelings! The Captain won't like that. She will probably want to kill you. Take them away!

LOST BOYS exit with SMEE, as if dragged off.

HOOK appears in the underground den looking at the sleeping PETER.

HOOK: Peter Pan. Look at you there, all tucked up under your little blanket, so serene and scrummy…I could eat you. We've had so much fun together, it's such a shame it has to finish. Nothing lasts forever though, always deep in the silence of the night you hear the tick tock and you know the end is coming. What do you care? Look at you, lying there with that smug little grin on your face and your tiresome baby teeth glinting in the moonlight. Even your sleep is cocky!

She goes to kill him with her hook, but stops herself.

HOOK: No. Too easy. I'm leaving you a gift.

HOOK puts poison into PETER's medicine bottle.

Make sure you drink up all your medicine. Night night Peter.

HOOK leaves. TINKER BELL appears, having seen what has just happened. She tries to wake PETER, panicked that she is too late. Finally he wakes.

TINKER BELL: O noo O noo O noo. Peta. Peta. Wek! *(Oh no oh no oh no. Peter. Peter. Wake up.)*

PETER: Tinker Bell? What are you doing here?

TINKER BELL: O noo. Hook! Ticky tocky ticky tocky ticky tocky. Chunka she bore! Meganna Losty Bys! Cannit Cannit, whoosh! *(Oh no. Hook! The tick tock. Big cow. And the Lost Boys. She got them. Got them. Took them away.)*

PETER: What? Hook has kidnapped Wendy and the Lost Boys?

TINKER BELL: Pretty boova. *(Big trouble.)*

PETER: Tinker Bell we must rescue them! First I must take my medicine!

TINKER BELL snatches it from him.

PETER: Tinker Bell! Give that back!

TINKER BELL: Noooo Peta, nooooo.

PETER: *(Replying in the TINKER BELL language.)* Peepers! Nak a mee meddygayth! *(Look, give me the medicine!)*

TINKER BELL forgets where she is for a moment, spell bound, and comes towards PETER. PETER grabs the bottle and a tug of war ensues. Eventually TINKER BELL drinks it. Immediately the poison starts taking effect.

TINKER BELL: Ha. O nooo. O nooo. Petrid. Hook. Ahhhhhh. Petrid. I wuv ooo Peieter. Ahhhh. I wuv ooo. Me morta. *(Ha!…Oh no. Oh no. It's poisoned. It's poisoned. Peter. I love you Peter. Ahhh. I love you. I'm dead.)*

TINKER BELL collapses on the floor, dead. PETER tries to revive her.

PETER: *(To the audience.)* Clap if you believe in fairies. Clap if you believe in fairies. Tinker Bell can you hear that? They believe in fairies!

He keeps repeating this until the audience starts clapping. He encourages them to clap and eventually TINKER BELL comes back to life and jumps into his arms.

PETER: Tinker Bell! She's alive! Don't you ever do that again!

TINKER BELL: O nooo. *(I won't.)*

PETER: And now to rescue Wendy!

They exit.

Act Five: The Pirate Ship

SCENE ONE: HOOK AND WENDY

The pirate ship comes in, SMEE at the wheel, the PIRATES singing a triumphant shanty.

HOOK:

> *Yo ho yo ho when she says claw,*
> *By fear they're overtook,*
> *Naught's left upon your bones when you,*
> *Have shaken hands with Hook.*
>
> *Yo ho yo ho The pirate life,*
> *The flag of skull and bones,*
> *A merry hour, a hempen rope,*
> *And a 'hey' for Davy Jones.*

The ship arrives in position.

HOOK: It is done. Smee, bring up the mother.

SMEE goes below leaving HOOK alone on deck.

HOOK: How still the night is. Nothing sounds alive. Now is the hour when children in their homes are a-bed, their lips bright-browned with the good night chocolate and their tongues drowsily searching for belated crumbs housed insecurely on their shining cheeks. Compare them with Peter Pan, now just a little dead boy. 'Tis my hour of triumph! And yet some disky spirit compels me to make my dying speech, lest when dying there may be no time for it...Oh Peter...The game's up.

SMEE comes up from below deck with WENDY.

HOOK: Welcome aboard the Jolly Roger. Won't you sit down? Let's have some tea.

SMEE brings tea.

HOOK: I'll be mother.

HOOK pours a cup of tea for WENDY.

HOOK: How are all the little ones? I hope they are getting some sleep. It's a big day for them. Walk the plank day. And there is nothing the little mother can do about it.

WENDY: It must be awful to be as lonely as you.

HOOK: Lonely? I am surrounded by a crew of obedient dogs who will do anything I say.

WENDY: They obey you but they don't really love you.

HOOK: My name is known throughout the world. Of course I am loved.

WENDY: If my mother were here she'd soon put a stop to all your nonsense. What you need is a jolly good bath and to be put to bed and to hear a jolly good story and then all your nightmares would fly away like little birds, back to where they came from.

HOOK: And then we'd all live happily ever after would we, little mother? Is that the sort of story you like?

WENDY: What other kind of story is there?

HOOK: Oh so young, so innocent. I'm afraid you're embarking upon your last chapter, entitled 'Wendy walks the plank.'

WENDY: If you think Peter will leave us here to die you're in for a very rude awakening.

HOOK: Poor Peter is dead, quite dead! Bring out the Lost Boys!

SCENE TWO: THE PIRATE SHIP

SMEE chases them up on deck.

SMEE: Tumble up you ungentlemanly lubbers!

The terrified boys are prodded up on to the deck.

HOOK: Listen to me you wretches! All of you miserable little children will die today, except one.

She kills the current cabin boy.

HOOK: I am looking for a new cabin boy. Who is interested in filling the position? What about you at the front there?

TOOTLES: I don't think my mother would like me to be a pirate. What about you, Curly?

CURLY: I actually think she'd be very disappointed. How about you Nibs?

NIBS: No my mother wouldn't like that. How about you-

HOOK: Stow your gab! *(Turning to MICHAEL.)* How about you boy, you look like you've got some pluck? Will you join us?

MICHAEL: What would you call me if I joined?

HOOK: Barnacle McGee.

MICHAEL: Can I visit home during the holidays?

HOOK: There won't be any holidays and this ship would be your home.

MICHAEL: What do you think John?

HOOK: Well John, what do you say?

JOHN: Would I ever see my mother again?

HOOK: I will be your mother. You can see me any time you like.

JOHN: Then I refuse.

MICHAEL and the other LOST BOYS join in with a general refusal.

HOOK: Then you die now. Starting with this one! Pray silence for a mother's last words to her children.

WENDY: Be brave boys. And remember your mothers always loved you.

HOOK: Is that it? Something of a disappointment. Get on the plank!-There is none can save you now!

PETER: There is one! Cock a doodle doo!

Suddenly PETER bursts out from inside the ship and flies into the air.

HOOK: Peter Pan! Alive?

The LOST BOYS all leap off the ship. HOOK points her gun at WENDY.

PETER: Leave her alone Hook, this is just between the two of us.

HOOK and PAN circle each other, all attention is on them. Meanwhile TIGER LILY scales the ship and jumps on SMEE. She sets WENDY free and wrestles SMEE down behind the ship, where she will staple him to the side.

HOOK: Proud and insolent youth, prepare to meet thy doom.

PETER: Dark and sinister woman, say your farewells.

HOOK: Take them to pieces boys! Kill them all!

The remaining PIRATES on the ship leap off and chase the LOST BOYS.

HOOK climbs up the mast to direct operations.

The LOST BOYS run round behind the ship and as they do so they collect pirate coats and become PIRATES.

Everyone is a PIRATE now. They stop, trying to sniff out the LOST BOYS.

Another circuit and they all turn into LOST BOYS.

They use the coats to be half PIRATE/half LOST BOY. They fight against themselves.

They whirl the coats above their heads so that we get the impression that the LOST BOYS are winning.

They throw the coats down and stamp on them. The PIRATES are all dead.

Focus turns to PETER and HOOK on the ship, building towards the final conflict.

HOOK is alone and aware that her end is close. She finds it hard to believe that PETER has defeated her.

HOOK: What are you, Peter Pan?

PETER: I am youth, I am joy. I am a little bird that has broken out of the egg.

The LOST BOYS have the mast encircled. There is no escape for HOOK. She throws down her weapon.

HOOK: Back you pewling spawn, I am the greatest pirate that ever lived and I am not going to be sent to my death at the hands of a bunch of whining children!

The LOST BOYS clear a pathway for her to get to the edge of the ship. The tick tock of the crocodile can be heard. Everyone stops to listen.

HOOK: Ah! That sweet sound, how timely. I care for no one and no one cares for me, but one thing I know; The basest of all things is to be afraid. When the last failing hand on the last miserable clock tick tocks and then stops on the final red evening of all time, there will still be one sound remaining. The echo of Hook's voice saying 'Step aside you lubbers. Fear will not stifle me. I am ready to depart.'

The crocodile is in the space now. It opens its mouth wide. HOOK dives into the water and is eaten. Once HOOK is dead the LOST BOYS cheer.

LOST BOYS:

> *We are the Lost Boys we live in Neverland,*
> *We got here some time ago, we fell out of our prams,*
> *We are the Lost Boys, brave soldiers all,*
> *Ready to do battle when we hear our Captain call,*
> *We are the Lost Boys, best of friends to some,*
> *We're as tough as leather and we're off to see our mums.*
> *We're off to see our mums …*
> *We're off to see our mums …*

PETER: Wendy set a course for the mainland.

WENDY: Ay ay Captain.

PETER: Second to the left and straight on till morning!

LOST BOYS:

> *We are the Lost Boys we live in Neverland,*
> *We got here some time ago, we fell out of our prams,*
> *We are the Lost Boys, brave soldiers all,*
> *Ready to do battle when we hear our Captain call,*
> *We are the Lost Boys, best of friends to some,*
> *We're as tough as leather and we're off to see our mums.*
> *We're off to see our mums …*
> *We're off to see our mums …*

More cheers as the pirate ship is wheeled back off stage.

SCENE THREE: THE RETURN HOME

MR and MRS DARLING push on the nursery bed. They collapse mournfully on it, berating themselves for the loss of their children, sobbing with regret.

MRS DARLING: I blame myself George. I should never have left them alone. What was I thinking?

MR DARLING: No, I am responsible for it all. I, George Darling, did it. I chained Nana in the yard and all because I was annoyed about the medicine. Oh mea culpa, mea culpa.

They collapse in tears and then fall asleep. The DARLINGS climb in through the window.

MICHAEL: John, I think I have been here before.

JOHN: Of course you have silly. Look there's our old bed. Hold on, there are people in it.

WENDY: It's Father and Mother

JOHN: So it is!

WENDY creeps over towards the bed.

MICHAEL: You weren't really our mother then, Wendy?

WENDY: No. Mother!

MRS DARLING thinks she is dreaming.

MRS DARLING: Wendy! There you are.

JOHN: Mother!

MRS DARLING: John.

MICHAEL: Mother!

MRS DARLING: Michael.

ALL: Mother we're home!

MRS DARLING is amazed and delighted to see the children.

MRS DARLING: George! Wake up! Our darlings are home!

They have a big hug all together on the bed. TOOTLES calls from outside on the window ledge.

TOOTLES: Wendy, we can't hold on to the drainpipe much longer.

WENDY: Come in all of you. It's alright Mother, they're just a few motherless boys we brought back with us.

The LOST BOYS trail in as MRS DARLING gets out of the bed.

WENDY: Please, please, say you'll have them!

MR DARLING: I must say Wendy, that you don't do things by halves.

TOOTLES: Do you think we should be too much of a handful, sir?

CURLY: Because if so we can actually go away.

NIBS: Or we could sleep doubled up.

WENDY: Please.

MRS DARLING: Of course we'll have them, won't we George?

MR DARLING: I dare say we could find space for you all in the drawing room, if you can be fitted in.

TOOTLES: We'll fit in sir.

MR DARLING: Mind you, I'm not sure that we have a drawing-room, but we pretend we do, and it's much the same thing. Then follow the leader!

BOYS: Follow the leader!

Everyone follows MR DARLING out, except WENDY and MRS DARLING, who hug each other. PETER is watching from the window ledge. WENDY becomes aware of him.

PETER: Cock a doodle doo. Hello Wendy.

WENDY: Hello Peter.

PETER: Goodbye Wendy.

WENDY: You don't have to go you know.

MRS DARLING walks over to PETER on the window ledge, trying to encourage him in.

MRS DARLING: Hello Peter. Why don't you come in? Join the family.

PETER: Would you send me to school?

MRS DARLING: Yes.

PETER: And then to an office?

MRS DARLING: I suppose so.

PETER: Then should I be a man?

MRS DARLING: Very soon.

PETER: No way lady! You're not going to catch me, make me go to school and learn solemn things. What if I was to wake up one morning and I'd grown a beard!

WENDY: Peter, I should love you in a beard.

PETER is momentarily distracted, thinking about himself with a beard. MRS DARLING approaches again.

PETER: Back away lady, no one's gonna catch me and make me a man.

WENDY: You'll be so lonely Peter.

PETER: Fly away with me.

WENDY: Mother may I?

MRS DARLING: Certainly not. I have her home again, and I mean to keep her.

WENDY: But he does so need a mother.

MRS DARLING: So do you my love, so do you.

PETER: Goodbye Wendy.

WENDY: Goodbye Peter. Don't forget.

PETER exits.

SCENE FOUR: AN AFTERTHOUGHT

MRS DARLING takes off her dressing gown and passes it to WENDY who puts it on, signifying the passage of time. As she does so, JANE enters and gets into the bed.

WENDY: And the last thing he ever said to me was 'Always be waiting' which was complete rubbish because he promptly forgot all about me.

JANE: Why did you never fly off and visit him?

WENDY: Because I can't. I've forgotten how.

JANE: Why have you forgotten?

WENDY: Because I'm not young and innocent and heartless. You have to be young and innocent and heartless to be able to fly.

JANE: I wish I was young and innocent and heartless. Mother, what did Peter's crow sound like?

WENDY: It sounded like this… *(She imitates the sound.)* Cock a doodle doo!!

JANE: No it didn't, it sounded like this.

Cock a doodle doo.

WENDY: How do you know that?

JANE: I often hear it when I am sleeping.

WENDY: Many girls hear it when they are sleeping, but I was the only one who heard it awake.

JANE: Lucky you.

WENDY: Come on! It's long past your bed time.

JANE: But I'm not tired.

WENDY: Well that's just tough luck.

> *It's not too late,*
> *Take these wings and fly,*
> *Away to your home.*

PETER enters on the ladder as WENDY sings the lullaby.

PETER: Cock a doodle doo. Hello Wendy.

WENDY: Peter.

PETER: Where is John?

WENDY: John isn't here.

PETER: Is Michael asleep?

WENDY: This isn't Michael.

PETER: Is it a new one?

WENDY: Yes.

PETER: Boy or girl?

WENDY: Girl.

PETER: Do you like her?

WENDY: Yes. Peter…you haven't come to ask me to fly away with you, have you?

PETER: Yes, come on. I'm Captain.

WENDY: I can't Peter. I've forgotten how to fly.

PETER: What is it?

WENDY: I will turn on the light.

PETER: Don't turn on the light.

WENDY: And then you can see for yourself.

PETER: Don't turn on the light. Don't turn on the light!

WENDY switches on the light.

WENDY: I grew up.

PETER: You promised not to!

WENDY: I did it long ago. I wanted to. And now I have a child.

PETER: No you don't.

WENDY: Yes I do. The little girl in the bed is my baby.

PETER: No she's not.

WENDY: Yes she is.

PETER: What does she call you?

WENDY: Mother

PETER falls off the ladder onto the floor, collapsing in a heap, sobbing.

WENDY: Oh Peter. Oh Peter.

JANE wakes up. The company begin to sing the lullaby.

JANE: Boy, why are you crying?

PETER: I wasn't crying.

JANE: It looked like you were crying

PETER bows. JANE bows.

PETER: What's your name?

JANE: Jane

PETER: My name is Peter Pan

JANE: Yes, I know. I've been waiting for you.

PETER: Fly away with me.

JANE: If you'll teach me how to fly, Peter. I've been practising but I can't quite do it yet.

PETER: What you need is a wonderful thought in your head. You'll also need fairy string.

JANE: Fairy string? Where do you get that from?

PETER: Tinker Bell's secret. The wonderful thought in your head will help to lift you!

JANE: Mother, watch this!

JANE flies up then lands. PETER does a somersault.

JANE: Mother I'm flying.

JANE does a double somersault.

JANE: Easy. Oh the cleverness of me!

PETER: Oh the cockiness of you. Now. Are you ready?

PETER and JANE fly together, holding hands.

WENDY: Jane! Remember, the window will always be open!

The rest of the company fly in the space.

THE END

PETER PAN

AND GREAT ORMOND STREET HOSPITAL

"All children, except one, grow up"

from Peter & Wendy
by J M Barrie

In 1929 J M Barrie gave the rights to his timeless classic *Peter Pan* to the Hospital for Sick Children at Great Ormond Street, which had opened its doors in 1852 with just 10 beds. It was the first children's hospital in the country.

Now known affectionately as GOSH, Great Ormond Street Hospital has 436 beds and the widest range of health services for children on one site in the UK.

The hospital still relies on the generosity of the public to help make it the extraordinary place it is today, giving hope to children who have the rarest, most complex and often life-threatening conditions.

Individual and corporate donations, along with performances of Peter Pan, continue to provide a vital resource to Great Ormond Street Hospital Children's Charity. The Charity helps GOSH pioneer new treatments, invest in state of the art equipment, care for young patients and their families and redevelop the hospital buildings, ensuring there are first-class facilities to match the hospital's world-class care.

To help transform childrens' lives, now and in the future, please visit **gosh.org/donate** or call **020 7341 3841** and talk to us about how you can get involved.

Great Ormond Street Hospital Charity

WWW.OBERONBOOKS.COM